Counseling Futures

Garry R. Walz
George M. Gazda
Bruce Shertzer

With a Preface by Tom Sweeney

Sponsored by Chi Sigma Iota

ERIC Counseling and Personnel Services Clearinghouse
2108 School of Education
The University of Michigan
Ann Arbor, MI 48109-1259

Copyright © 1991 by ERIC Counseling and Personnel Services Clearinghouse

All rights reserved.

ERIC Counseling and Personnel Services Clearinghouse
2108 School of Education
The University of Michigan
Ann Arbor, Michigan 48109-1259

Cover design and publication layout by Patricia Wisner

Editorial by Penny Schreiber

ISBN 1-56109-005-0

This publication was prepared with partial funding from the Office of Educational Research and Improvement, U.S. Department of Education under contract no. RI88062011. The opinions expressed in this report do not necessarily reflect the positions or policies of OERI, the Department of Education, or ERIC/CAPS.

Dedication

This book is dedicated to

C. Gilbert Wrenn

who by his own example
has inspired counselors around the world
to anticipate the future and celebrate change

Table of Contents

Introduction vii
  Garry R. Walz

Preface ix
  Tom Sweeney

About the Authors xi

Chapter 1. Some Basic Conceptions
  Regarding a Study of the Future 1
  Garry R. Walz

Chapter 2. What Recent Survey Research
  Indicates for the Future of Counseling
  and Counselor Education 11
  George M. Gazda

Chapter 3. The Evolution of Counseling 27
  Bruce Shertzer

Chapter 4. Forces for Change in Counseling
  and Counselor Education 39
  Garry R. Walz

Chapter 5. Nine Trends Which Will Affect
  the Future of the United States 61
  Garry R. Walz

Chapter 6. Future Focused Generalizations
  on Counseling 71
  Garry R. Walz

References 79

ERIC/CAPS 85

Introduction

There are—at the very least—as many possible futures as there are people.
—**Anonymous**

The old adage "to be forewarned is to be forearmed" is one that ERIC/CAPS has long subscribed to. Acquiring quality information prior to making important decisions is "to be forewarned," and using the best available information in carrying out important actions and plans is "to be forearmed." Access to cutting edge information, be it from research and development or policy makers, is vital to effective functioning, to professional viability in an information society.

Information, no matter how vital or comprehensive, may be more cumbersome than capacitating unless it is in response to important goals. Like the person who buys things because "...it was such a terrific bargain," unless you have important goals or know what you need or want, you may end up with a lot of information that you don't need, even wish you didn't have.

That's where futuring, or more appropriately, *imaging* the future, becomes important. It helps you to reflect on, to prepare for events before their occurrence. And that is why ERIC/CAPS has a long history of developing publications and offering programs and conferences in futuring and counseling (see the reference section for some examples). Perhaps the most notable example was the collaboration between ERIC/CAPS and ACES which led to the EPCOT publication and conference—*The Experimental Prototype of the Counselor of Tomorrow* (Walz & Benjamin, 1983).

This publication grew out of the leadership of Tom Sweeney and the Chi Sigma Iota program on the Future of Counseling offered in conjunction with the ACES National Conference in St. Louis. In addition to the papers which were drafted after the conference by Dr. George Gazda, Dr. Bruce Shertzer and Dr. Garry Walz, a number of additional sections were developed to aid the user in reflecting and acting upon their images of the future. We are delighted to have our comrades in arms, the Chi Sigma Iota, sponsor this monograph and join with us in encouraging counselors to "study" the future.

It is, in my judgment, absolutely true that "...there are at least as many possible futures as there are people." This monograph is intended to help you in constructing your own counseling futures so you can better prepare yourself for the future you envisage.

Happy futuring! With luck our futures will include the opportunity to be together and share our thoughts and feelings about the future.

Garry R. Walz
Director, ERIC/CAPS

Preface

Chi Sigma Iota Counseling Academic and Professional Honor Society, established in 1985, now has over 5,400 members and 100 chapters in this country and abroad. Conceived as a society of professional counselors dedicated to excellence in preparation and practice, it has sponsored a number of successful activities at both the chapter and international levels.

In conjunction with the National Board of Certified Counselors (NBCC), CSI developed and helps to distribute a brochure which is frameable for use in counselors' offices on "client rights and responsibilities." This brochure was sent to syndicated columnists, licensing boards, chairs of counselors education departments as well as all members of CSI and NCC's. It is available at cost through NBCC.

The Society has twelve distinguished scholars who donate their time to speak at chapter functions. These include George Gazda, Joann Harris-Bowlsbey, John Holland, Kenneth Hoyt, John Krumboltz, Bruce Shertzer, Donald Super, Thelma Jones Vriend, Garry Walz, Clemmont Vontress, C. Gilbert Wrenn, and George Wright. Some of these scholars have already given speeches at the CSI theme sessions "Scholars Across the Generations" at the AACD conventions, and the ACES National Convention in St. Louis on the "Future of Counseling" was the impetus for the ERIC/CAPS Counseling Futures monograph. In more than one case, the scholars' efforts have helped chapters establish scholarship and related funds for local use by the membership.

The Society also sponsors awards for excellence in research, academic pursuits and chapter activities.

This year, in conjunction with chapter and society contributions, we are again awarding ten fellowships of $200 each for future leaders to attend the AACD Convention and a special leadership training program conducted by CSI President-Elect and AACD Past-President Rose Cooper. These awardees will also participate in the CSI business and recognition/initiation functions, and two will be selected as CSI interns to work closely with the President and Executive Director on special projects.

Currently, AACD staff are helping the Society establish a CSI Scholars Library Section in the AACD Headquarters Library. In addition to ensuring that all the major works of the CSI scholars are available to all members of the profession, the CSI Executive Council plans to make annual contributions to the AACD Library.

The Society also is offering three awards from the ERIC/CAPS Center to further the research of deserving members of the Society. Awardees will receive $100, $75 or $50 certificates for materials or reference searches through ERIC/CAPS.

For more information on membership or how to establish a chapter contact: Dr. Tom Sweeney, Executive Director, Chi Sigma Iota, 313C McCracken Hall, Ohio University, Athens, OH 45701.

Tom Sweeney
Executive Director
Chi Sigma Iota

About the Authors

Garry R. Walz, Ph.D., is Director of the ERIC Counseling and Personnel Services Clearinghouse and Professor of Higher and Adult Continuing Education at The University of Michigan in Ann Arbor. He is a past chair of the Department of Guidance and Counseling and the director of numerous funded research and development projects and training institutes in counseling and human services. A prolific author, he has also served as President of the American Personnel and Guidance Association and the Association for Counselor Education and Supervision. He was honored in 1988 as a Distinguished Scholar by Chi Sigma Iota and was previously awarded the coveted Kathleen and Gilbert Wrenn Humanitarian Award.

George M. Gazda, Ed.D., is Research Professor in the Department of Counseling and Human Development Services and Acting Associate Dean for Research in the College of Education at the University of Georgia in Athens. In addition, he is Clinical Professor in the Department of Psychiatry at the Medical College of Georgia. Dr. Gazda is past president of many associations including the American Personnel and Guidance Association and the Association for Specialists in Group Work (which he co-founded). He is the author, co-author or editor of numerous books and has published widely in professional counseling journals. He frequently acts as a consultant for national and international organizations and universities and has been the recipient of many awards for research and service.

Bruce Shertzer is Professor of Counseling and Development and Head of the Department of Educational Studies at Purdue University in West Lafayette, Indiana. He is a trustee of the American Association of Counseling and Development Foundation and a past chairman of that organization. In 1986 the American Association for Counseling and Development bestowed on him their Distinguished Professional Service Award. He is author or co-author of a dozen textbooks, editor or co-editor of 100 monographs, and author of more than 50 journal articles.

Chapter 1

Some Basic Conceptions Regarding a Study of the Future

Garry R. Walz

How individuals view the future depends in part on the methods they use to access the future. Each methodology has its own strengths and contributions but also its limitations and/or special perspective. Among the more commonly used methods are the following:

Writer/Artistic Perceptions of the Future

The most imaginative perceptions of the future are those of writers and artists who typically give free reign to their creative processes unfretted by data analysis or other constraining forces. Not infrequently writers such as Jules Verne, Aldous Huxley, and H. G. Wells, as well as numerous science fiction writers, will foresee future events in great clarity long before they occurred to others. In many instances, the visions of writers have proved to be precursors of actual events and developments. Because they do not feel a need to be held to the present "facts," futuristic writers can offer a vision that is surprising in its scope and the accuracy of characterization when later compared with actual developments.

How individuals view the future depends in part on the methods they use to access the future.

...the visions of [fiction] writers have proved to be precursors of actual events and developments.

Demographic Images of the Future

Demographics provide detailed and clearcut images of some aspects of the future such as what the age and racial composition of our population will be at a given point in time. In imaging the future demographics has one distinct advantage over all the other methods—it speaks to what exists and is now present and does not involve guesswork or tenuous projections. We can speak with great clarity as to how many high school students there will be in a decade because those students are now in elementary school. By carefully analyzing census demographic data we can describe future needs and conditions with an accuracy unparalleled by other methods. It is therefore an indispensable tool in fashioning images of the future.

Megatrends

First developed as a tool for military intelligence, megatrends identifies trends or developments in our society in a few key early adoption and high influence areas (such as Florida and California, and to some extent in other areas as well) where what is occurring now can be seen as a precursor of trends that will spread across the entire country. Because megatrends references trends that are already evident, this methodology possesses some of the advantages of demographics (Naisbitt, 1982). The potential for error in this method derives from generalizing about American society as a whole based on isolated pockets of new trends.

Futurist Perspective

In a literal sense futurists are not seers or forecasters. They are not interested in prophesizing what events or developments will occur by a specific date. Instead they wish to study alternative futures giving attention to possible and probable futures. A favorite tool is to develop future scenarios where given conditions and developments or multiple scenarios or dynamic descriptions of certain aspects of our culture are presented for analysis and discussion and future planning. A preferred time perspective for futuristic planning is the middle term future—a period five to ten years hence. A shorter time period offers no great advantage for intensive study, and a time period of over 10 years presents real hazards for developing viable future images and scenarios.

Future Shock

Alvin Toffler (1972), the originator of the term "future shock," is a futurist who has devoted himself to the study of change and its impact on human lives. It is his central thesis that the acceleration of change is so great that unless man learns to control the rate of change in his personal affairs as well as in society at large, he will be doomed to massive adoptational breakdowns. His goal is to help people cope more effectively with personal and social change by better understanding how man responds to change and how we can develop a strategy of adoption. Unlike many futurists who focus exclusively on the direction of change Toffler believes that the rate of change has important implications, perhaps more important than the direction of change.

Seers and Assorted Soothsayers

Throughout time individuals ranging from tea readers and fortune tellers to famous prophets have claimed to be able to foretell the future. While both the accuracy and the utility of their predictions are often in serious doubt, they have nonetheless contributed to an interest in predicting and analyzing the future. Many persons who originally had their appetite for thinking about the future whetted by soothsayers have gone on to more serious and substantive study of the future.

A preferred time perspective for futuristic planning is the middle term future—a period five to ten years hence.

His goal [A. Toffler's] is to help people cope more effectively with personal and social change by better understanding how man responds to change and how we can develop a strategy of adoption....Toffler believes the rate of change has important implications, perhaps more important than the direction of change.

This brief and modest review of different approaches to thinking about and viewing the future is not intended to be either comprehensive or definitive. Rather, it is intended to provide a brief glimpse of the different methodologies that exist for coming to know the future and the nature of the views or images each will project.

Futuring Concepts

Listed below are six concepts regarding a study of the future. They are intended to assist readers in better understanding future analyses and how to use them.

1. How we access and view the future depends to a rather large extent on the methods we use.

A demographer may have a clear and distinct view of the future based on present knowns, while a futurist may present a number of alternative images of the future and the implications inherent in each of them for people in both the present and the future. Both views are valuable. The real challenge is to be able to utilize the unique perspective presented by each to develop meaningful generalizations about the future and to draw out the important implications of the generalizations for counseling.

> *The real challenge is to be able to utilize the unique perspective presented by each [futuristic method] to develop meaningful generalizations about the future and to draw out the important implications of the generalizations for counseling.*

2. How we view the future not only affects how we prepare for it, but also has a profound effect upon how we act in the present.

Perhaps one of the reasons that many people dismiss futuristic discussions as "fun and fantasy" is that they see such ruminations as beyond any present significance. "Why should I be talking about something ten years hence when I can't even get a firm grip on daily problems and challenges?" could well be said by many to explain their seeming reluctance to devote time to discussing the future. In reality, our perceptions and feelings of what the future will bring can have a profound effect upon how we view and act in the *present*. Counselor educators who view life as stable and tranquil with few major challenges or changes will focus their efforts upon programs that emphasize known truths and accumulated experiences. They will emphasize the refinement and improvement of present counseling methods and procedures. Conversely, counselor educators who view the future as something that will bring major challenges and changes are more likely to monitor societal developments to assess new counseling emphases. Information access, professional renewal and change agentry would be major nutritional items on the plates of counselor educators who anticipate significant changes in the short- or middle-term future. Thus, two counselor educators who are similar in their views about theories and procedures in counseling could nonetheless act very differently when instructing or supervising counselors if their perceptions of the future are at variance with one another. (Interestingly, many of the seemingly circular discussions about goals and priorities in counseling would be minimized if we were more communicative regarding our views of the future.) In our efforts to understand the expressed views and priorities of a particular counselor educator we need to address their concepts of and feelings about the future as much as we need to analyze the logic of their stated views.

> *...our perceptions and feelings of what the future will bring can have a profound effect upon how we view and act in the present.*

> *...two counselor educators who are similar in their views about theories and procedures in counseling could nonetheless act very differently when instructing or supervising counselors if their perceptions of the future are at variance with one another.*

3. **Persons who intensively reflect upon and study the future frequently experience a tempering phenomenon—they pull back from apparently justified expressions of major change and settle for expressing more conservative less radical expressions of change.**

In the act of discovery of "new truth" it is a common phenomenon for the discoverer to be surprised or even startled by the departure of his/her findings from conventional wisdom. Particularly on topics where the data relevant to a particular inquiry are diffuse or even contradictory, a new finding strongly at variance from an accepted or expected finding may give the discoverer pause: "Is this right?" "Did I analyze the data correctly?" "Why are my findings such a departure from what others have found?" Several futurists I have personally known have confided in me that they softened their findings, suggesting more modest change than was suggested by their analyses. In an informal discussion of megatrends, Naisbitt (1982) expressed the view that were he to do it again he would have been bolder in his descriptions of how society would change. Like many engaged in future studies he pulled back from his most "far out" findings and presented sanitized, less radical trends. Out of fear of being wrong or subject to ridicule, it is not uncommon for a futurist to hedge his future bets. While pulling back may provide us with a greater sense of security it also can dampen the strength of our findings and lead to homogenized findings that are palatable but lacking in the spice that can cause a readjustment on the thinking and behaving of others.

Out of fear of being wrong or subject to ridicule, it is not uncommon for a futurist to hedge his future bets.

4. **The actual process of futurizing, e.g., of reflecting upon the changes that can/may occur and what implications those changes can have for a society, may be as valuable as the findings which result.**

It has been said that strategic planning benefits an organization not only because it results in an actual strategic plan but also because it causes people to drop old ways of thinking and come to grips with matters that have for too long been pushed aside or ignored. A process which assists people to rethink previously held values and beliefs and to move their time perspective from the present to tomorrow is no small accomplishment.

A process which assists people to rethink previously held values and beliefs and to move their time perspective from the present to tomorrow is no small accomplishment.

Similarly, counselor educators who engage in intensive reflection and discussion about the future of counseling may be as far from a consensus as to what the future will be at the end of their discussion as when they began. But the process of thinking about tomorrow and the demands it will place on counselors is fully justified because it leads to thinking about counseling with a fresh perspective and with a new set of goals and outcomes in mind. Whether the outcome is program change or constancy is not the issue—rather that what we do is *future tested*, that we have examined what we are doing in counselor education and why we are doing it in the light of what we believe the future will demand of us.

...the process of thinking about tomorrow and the demands it will place on counselors is fully justified because it leads to thinking about counseling with a fresh perspective and with a new set of goals and outcomes in mind.

5. A major difficulty is the intellectual nature of the futurizing process and the consistent failure on the part of those engaged in futurizing to internalize and act upon the conclusions they reach.

It can be said that the future is akin to the weather—it is something we all talk about but don't do anything about. As a discussion topic, the future of counseling has unlimited potential for either serious discourse or cocktail banter. Fine. But the payoff comes in using the insights gained from the study and discussion in concrete and viable programmatic changes. Like an inspiring and captivating speech, futures discussions devoid of commitment to change and action are satisfying but hardly helpful. The very nature of the topic seems to engender more than the usual amount of rhetoric over response. If the prelude (talk) becomes the "pastlude" by default then futures discussions may be more hurtful than helpful by giving the participants a false sense of futureness and reduce any felt need for further discussion or changes in counselor education program planning and action taking.

Like an inspiring and captivating speech, futures discussions devoid of commitment to change and action are satisfying but hardly helpful.

6. Our goal should not be to attempt to predict or forecast what the future will be but rather to identify possible and probable futures and then work towards what we believe to be our preferred future.

In a real sense it is impossible to know the future. Forecasting what the future will bring is at best difficult. More importantly, an emphasis on predicting the future, on "being right" can easily lead to a reactive stance. If great effort is put into forecasting events and conditions then not surprisingly the range of program options will be narrowed to those seen as responding to the predicted trends and events.

A more desirable approach is to identify what are possible futures (the range of different events and outcomes which can occur) and probable futures (what are the events more likely to occur). Given a knowledge of what is possible and probable it is possible to bend all of one's efforts towards achieving that which is most desired. What is likely or not likely to be experienced in the future is important only in so much as it informs the respondents as to the magnitude and/or difficulty of the task. It does not specifically direct the choice of priority or goal. The inherent value of and need for the choice is basic to what future choices are made.

...an emphasis on predicting the future, on "being right" can easily lead to a reactive stance.

Given a knowledge of what is possible and probable it is possible to bend all of one's efforts towards achieving that which is most desired.

Summary

We have suggested that six factors can play an important role in our approach to futurizing. Each of the six factors is important in its own right but taken together they exert a potent force upon the future-oriented behavior of a profession or an individual program.

First, we suggested that the means used to access the future can determine whether the future is seen as inviting or hostile, desirable or enigmatic, predictable or random (e.g., demographics, forecasting, megatrends, etc.). Dissimilar means for accessing the future are likely to produce dissimilar concepts of the future with implications and consequences for counseling.

Second, it was noted that the images we create of the future will likely be as important for their effect upon our behavior in the present as well as in the future. We may conjecture as to how we will behave in the future based upon our present views but our futuristic views will have immediate and visible effects upon our behavior in the present. Even though we may be skeptical of the futuring process and how accurate our visions of the future can be, it is nonetheless important that attention be given to views and feelings about the future for the implications it has for present counseling priorities and goals.

Third, note was made of the natural tendency when futuring to temper and downplay future images that were at variance with conventional wisdom for fear of being seen as outlandish or foolish. Initially audacious and innovative views can be expected to be bombarded by dissenting conventionality.

Fourth, it was suggested that the end results of futuring may not be as important as the process of struggling with and arriving at a vision of the future. A counselor education program, an individual counselor, or even an entire profession that grapples with what it believes to be their future will be all the wiser and more strategically positioned for the effort itself, irrespective of whether it produces consensus or a specific document.

Fifth, caution was raised about an all too human predilection to equate unexamined expression of feelings with substantive exploration and dissection of significant concepts. The greatest benefit will accrue to those individuals and programs who internalize the insights and ideas gained from the futuring process and who seek specific means to take action on their ideas.

Sixth, finally and perhaps most importantly, both as individual counselors and as a profession we need to consider the differences between responding in a

...both as individual counselors and as a profession we need to consider the differences between responding in a reactive way to future forecasts as contrasted with a proactive stance that focuses upon making a preferred future happen and become a living reality.

reactive way to future forecasts as contrasted with a proactive stance that focuses upon making a preferred future happen and become a living reality.

Chapter 2

What Recent Survey Research Indicates for the Future of Counseling and Counselor Education

George M. Gazda

Trends in Counseling—Survey One

I shall summarize three surveys regarding trends in counseling and counselor education taken since 1980 and then cite what I would like to see occur for counseling in the future. The first survey was conducted and reported by Daniel and Weikel (1983) in the *Personnel and Guidance Journal.* This survey used the Delphi method and was based on an original response rate of 26% of 334 full-time doctoral level faculty randomly chosen from approximately 1600 listed in *Counselor Preparation 1980* (Hollis & Wantz, 1986). The first mailing of the survey was made in February 1981. The 86 respondents (26%) generated 48 trend statements. The second mailing to the 86 respondents produced a return rate of 79%. The second survey requested opinions concerning the probability of occurrence and the predicted time frame of the forecast statements. The third and final mailing to the original 86 respondents produced an 80% response rate. During this survey the mean and modes for each of the trend statements from the second survey were

I shall summarize three surveys regarding trends in counseling and counselor education taken since 1980 and then cite what I would like to see occur for counseling in the future.

provided. The respondents were requested to predict probability and time frame with the data provided.

In the data analysis, means were used to determine rank order of the statements by probability of occurrence. Modes were used to determine trend statement probability consensus and time frame consensus. Standard deviations were used to indicate agreement among respondents. Tables 1, 2, and 3 summarize the survey results. They are reproduced from *The Personnel and Guidance Journal* with permission from the American Association of Counseling and Development. Trends predicted in Tables 1–3 can be compared with the next two surveys for confirmation or disconfirmation.

Trends in Courses, Degrees and Programs, Administration, Accreditation, Graduates, Employment, Faculty, Practicum and Internship, Admissions, and Financial Assistance—Survey Two

Survey Two includes data from 493 of 582 identified administrative units offering counselor preparation programs reported in *Counselor Preparation 1986–89: Programs, Personnel, Trends* (Hollis and Wantz, 1986). The following table and summaries are reproduced with permission of Accelerated Development, Inc.

Courses

Table 4 illustrates the top six most frequently added courses for the 1984–87 period. The number of courses dropped for 1984–87 was insignificant and shows no trend.

Table 1
"Highly Probable" Trends in Counseling and Predicted Time of Occurrence

Rank Order	Probability		Trend Statement	Time Frame	
	Mean	N		Mode	N
1	1.368	68	There will be an increase in gerontological counseling as a specialty	1981–85	62
2	1.397	68	There will be a new emphasis on career counseling through the life span	1981–85	60
3	1.403	67	Emphasis on counseling through the life span will increase	1981–85	60
4	1.426	68	There will be an increase in counseling with adult populations	1981–85	59
5	1.435	69	There will be an increased emphasis on the accreditation of counselor education programs	1981–85	62
6	1.449	69	There will be an increased emphasis on continuing and in-service education for counselors	1981–85	60
7	1.500	68	There will be an increase in mental health counseling as a specialty	1981–85	54
8	1.562	67	There will be increased use of computers and other technological advances by counselors	1981–85	58
9	1.556	68	Federal and state funds for counseling services will continue to decrease	1981–85	58
10	1.567	67	There will be an emphasis on counseling for special groups (i.e., minorities, women, marriage, divorced parents)	1981–85	61
11	1.581	62	A focus on preventive activities in counseling will be emphasized	1981–85	52

Table 2
Probable Trends in Counseling and Predicted Time of Occurrence

Rank Order	Probability			Trend Statement	Time Frame	
	Mean	N			Mode	N
1	1.582	57		There will be greater emphasis on the counselor's role as a consultant to parents, teachers, and others	1981–85	62
2	1.588	68		There will be more emphasis on counselor accountability	1981–85	61
3	1.638	69		There will be an increased emphasis on post-masters training in specialty areas (i.e., marriage, family, adult, alcohol)	1986–90	61
4	1.642	67		Journals in the counseling field will become fewer and more expensive to produce	1986–90	58
5	1.691	68		Counseling services will be provided to a greater extent within business and industry	1986–90	59
6	1.716	67		There will be an increase in the use of media technology (i.e., television, recorders, telephone) in the delivery of counseling services	1981–85	54
7	1.750	68		Professional counselors will supervise increasing numbers of peer counselors and paraprofessionals	1986–90	55
8[a]	1.791	67		There will be an increased emphasis on holistic models of counseling	1981–85	57
9[a]	1.791	67		There will be an increase in cognitive-behavioral approaches to counseling	1981–85	58
10[a]	1.791	67		Group counseling will be utilized to a greater extent	1981–85	52
11	1.826	69		Masters level training will consist of 60 semester hours with increased field experience	1986–90	53

[a]For simplicity, these three tied rank items were arbitrarily given consecutive rank order numbers.

Table 2 (continued)
Probable Trends in Counseling and Predicted Time of Occurrence

Rank Order	Probability		Trend Statement	Time Frame	
	Mean	N		Mode	N
12	1.851	68	Counseling will become increasingly multidisciplinary	1986–90	54
13	1.882	68	Counselors will be required to be certified or licensed by most states	1986–90	55
14	1.926	68	Use of peer counseling will increase	1981–85	48
15	1.940	67	Counselors will be included in a national registry	1986–90	52
16	1.957	69	There will be a decrease in the number of counselor education programs	1981–85	54
17	1.985	67	There will be an increased awareness of chemical aspects and use of chemotherapy in the control of behavior	1986–90	50
18	2.000	68	Counseling services will shift to more private practices and clinics	1986–90	54
19	2.015	67	Fewer counselors will be employed by the schools	1981–85	44
20	2.029	68	Counseling will be widely accepted as a profession	1986–90	55
21	2.045	67	There will be a continued movement toward a systems approach to counseling	1986–90	49
22	2.059	68	Counseling services will shift from the public school to other community based providers	1986–90	47
23	2.088	68	The faculty of counselor education programs will be required to be licensed/certified and/or psychologists	1986–90	44
24	2.101	69	There will be an increased emphasis on doctoral level training	1986–90	45

Table 2 (continued)
Probable Trends in Counseling and Predicted Time of Occurrence

Rank Order	Probability Mean	N	Trend Statement	Time Frame Mode	N
25	2.118	68	Increasing numbers of paraprofessional counselors will be trained in undergraduate or special programs	1986–90	49
26	2.136	66	Counseling research will expand and professional organizations will organize task forces to improve research	1986–90	43
27	2.162	68	Competency based standards will be employed in the certification and/or licensure of counselors	1986–90	48
28	2.176	68	Use of paraprofessionals in counseling will increase	1981–85	42
29	2.261	69	Counselor education programs will shift toward becoming counseling psychology programs	1986–90	42
30	2.269	67	More professional alliances will form and some existing APGA, APA, and NRA divisions will merge	1986–90	40
31	2.303	66	Several divisions will secede from APGA	1986–90	37
32	2.420	69	Masters level counselors will become less employable	1981–85	35
33	2.529	68	Counselors will become eligible for third party payments from insurance and/or government carriers	1986–90	35

Table 3
Improbable Trends in Counseling

Rank Order	Probability Mean	N	Trend Statement
1	2.448	67	There will be more growth in elementary school guidance and counseling services with more states mandating elementary counselors
2	2.515	66	There will be a change in the role of the school counselor with that role emphasizing "student counseling"
3	2.609	69	There will be a shift of preparation programs from the university setting toward community settings (i.e., agencies, business, and industry)
4	2.899	69	There will be less distinction and less "turfism" among mental health professionals as they merge into a related corps of helping professionals

Table 4
Rank Order of the Top Six Courses Added in 1984–1987 (1986 Data)

Rank	Content Area	#
1	Marriage & Family Counseling	112
2	Substance Abuse	101
3	Legal & Ethical Issues	52
4	Career & Life Planning	41
5	Multicultural Counseling	40
6	Consultation	35
	Total	381

Degrees and Programs

Degree and program changes based on 1986 data are occurring but are few in number. The Ph.D. degree continues to increase in comparison to the Ed.D. Counseling Psychology was the most frequently listed addition to program changes in majors. A corresponding increase appears to be occurring in the number of programs that are dropping counseling and guidance degrees/programs in education. Other trends are as follows:

1. The number of hours required to complete programs is increasing and correspondingly the one-year graduate program for counselor preparation is disappearing.
2. The generic term "counseling" is being modified by the addition of prefixes such as "mental health," "marriage and family," "school," etc., and likewise more than one major at the master's degree level is being offered.
3. Rehabilitation counseling is decreasing in offerings.

The Ph.D. degree continues to increase in comparison to the Ed.D.

The generic term "counseling" is being modified by the addition of prefixes such as "mental health," "marriage and family," "school," etc. . . .

Administration

The titles of administrative units were found to be continuing to change but not as much as reported in the 1983 data. Causal factors were not determined through the survey. An increased number of programs are being discontinued, the majority of which were those preparing school counselors.

Accreditation

Accreditation is continuing to increase with APA, CACREP, CAMFTE, and CORE leading the way. In 1983, CACREP had accredited a total of 22 programs compared with 47 in 1986; whereas APA had accredited a total of 37 counseling psychology programs in 1983 and 47 in 1986. AAMFT (CAMFTE) had accredited 13 programs in 1983 and 34 by 1986. Consistent with the decrease in rehabilitation programs, CORE had accredited 76 programs in 1983 versus 75 in 1986.

The increasing emphasis on accreditation is affecting programs by determining the program content more than faculty determine it. Likewise, accreditation standards are affecting titles in majors by reducing them in number. Also, minimum criteria reflected through accreditation standards are becoming maximum standards for programs. Overall, the trend is toward more counselor education programs seeking accreditation.

Graduates

The following trends in the number and kinds of graduates have been determined:

1. The ratio of women to men (with the exception of student personnel in higher education) is approximately 3 to 2 and indications are that it will continue at this rate.

The increasing emphasis on accreditation is affecting programs by determining the program content more than faculty determine it.

The ratio of women to men (with the exception of student personnel in higher education) is approximately 3 to 2 and indications are that it will continue at this rate.

2. Full-time equivalent faculty has begun to show a decrease since 1980 with a corresponding increase in nonprofessional ranks such as adjunct, visiting, and lecturer. This trend may be reflected in the increasing numbers of site supervisors of practica and internships who are being given faculty status.

Practicum and Internship

The average number of clock hours required for practicum and internship shows a continuing increase....

The average number of clock hours required for practicum and internship shows a continuing increase and, although non-accredited programs are increasing their required clock hours, theirs are still less than accredited programs. Clock hour requirements for practicum and internship continue to vary depending upon function and setting, but there is a shift toward more requirements being completed in settings similar to students' projected employment. However, a shift in settings has occurred without a change in accountability of the counselor preparation administrative units. The trend, also, is for internship site personnel to do the supervision at the doctoral level except for marriage and family interns. Psychology related degree programs rely more heavily on site personnel to do the supervision than do other program emphases. Inasmuch as the trend is for more practicum and internship placement and supervision to be done outside the department, it is expected that accreditation of practicum and internship sites will become a necessity.

Inasmuch as the trend is for more practicum and internship placement and supervision to be done outside the department, it is expected that accreditation of practicum and internship sites will become a necessity.

Admissions

Summarized below are the trends and/or conditions of admissions requirements:

1. The most frequently used standardized test is the Graduate Record Examination (GRE).
2. For doctoral programs, the GRE total average is approximately 1000 with 500 verbal and 500 quantitative. (Doctoral program requirements

are higher than for master's and verbal requirements are slightly higher than quantitative.) The minimum test score required often depends upon other admissions information such as a high GPA in coursework which may be a compensation for lower test scores.
3. In addition to test scores other criteria are being required for admission. These criteria vary widely from institution to institution but there is a trend of requiring two or more items from the following: prior work experience, interviews, prior courses, prior GPA, and letters of recommendation. Of these items just cited, prior number of courses in areas such as psychology and/or counseling continues to vary considerably from program to program; GPA averages in both undergraduate and graduate courses vary significantly from program to program; letters of recommendation are increasingly being used by programs and three letters seems to be the typical number required; interviews are increasingly being required; work experience is becoming an admissions requirement factor with doctoral programs in general requiring two years and master's programs requiring from one to two years.

... there is a trend [for admission] of requiring two or more items from the following: prior work experience, interviews, prior courses, prior GPA, and letters of recommendation.

Financial Assistance

Financial assistance continues to be made available with increasing dollar amounts. Assistantships, loans, and fellowships in that order of frequency are the major sources of financial aid.

Trends in Faculty Positions Turnover—Survey Three

Survey Three was completed and published by White and Hernandez (1988) in *Counselor Education and*

Supervision. A 25% random sample of faculty was taken from Hollis and Wantz directories of 1971–74, 1980–83, and 1986–89. The survey covered a 15-year period from 1971–1986. The sample consisted of 72 publicly funded and 22 privately funded institutions (62 granted masters degrees and 32 granted both masters and doctoral degrees). Data for a six-year projection period were collected from the 94 departments. They were asked to project full-time equivalent (FTE) departures for the periods 1987–89 and 1990–92 and to establish absolute gains and losses for each period. The results are summarized as follows:

Faculty Trends 1971–86

1. Both transitional volatility and overall department size tended to decrease in the 1980's.

Faculty Projections 1987–1992

1. Slightly less than one-half of the programs (47.6%) regardless of size, were projected to have one or more faculty departures between 1987–89 and 64.2% between 1990–92. (The most frequently expected departure was 1.0 FTE.)
2. Projected *absolute* changes by institution's funding basis showed no differences. (Most chairpersons hoped to maintain FTE faculty size.)

Trends for Women

1. The percentage of women in counselor education departments increased quite steadily from 10.7% in 1971 to 26.1% in 1986. Women also seem to have substantially greater prospects of finding positions in counselor education in the next few years.

The percentage of women in counselor education departments increased quite steadily from 10.7% in 1971 to 26.1% in 1986.

Other Trends

1. Faculty members in counselor education were becoming older from 1971–1986—similar to other disciplines.
2. Tenure-eligible positions were predicted to be essentially unchanged for 1987–1990 and 1990–1992.

License Importance

1. Persons preparing for counselor education faculty positions will be at a substantial disadvantage without license eligibility.

Mobility of Counselor Educators

1. Program departure from 1974–83 showed that 8 of every 9 persons who left a faculty position apparently left counselor education as an occupation.
2. The probability of relocating to another counselor education program tends to decrease as the presence in one program continues.

In summary, (1) the percentage of women in counselor education increased by 2 1/2 times since 1971 and further increases seem to be virtually certain; (2) a very mild increase in positions over losses is projected more for 1990–92 than for 1987–89; (3) if projections prove to be true, counselor education as an occupation and as a higher education discipline may be stabilized.

> From the point of view of a person with aspirations to become a counselor educator, data developed here suggest some basis for optimism, but some cautions as well. Prospects for entry seem to be improving, especially for women, and very definitely for persons eligible for some sort of a practitioner license.... With

Persons preparing for counselor education faculty positions will be at a substantial disadvantage without license eligibility.

Program departure from 1974–83 showed that 8 of every 9 persons who left a faculty position apparently left counselor education as an occupation.

only about 1 in 5 people who left counselor education over the most recent 6-year period doing so to retire, planning only to be a counselor educator would seem to be very risky. (White & Hernandez, 1988, p. 87)

What Gazda Would Like to See for Counseling in the Future

First: Much better training programs with more comprehensive training and higher skill levels.

To accomplish this will require fewer but better staffed and regulated programs, better selection of trainees, longer training programs, greater use of technology, increased use of competency in evaluating skills development.

Second: More and better research on process and outcomes in counseling with increased replications

To accomplish this will require more interdisciplinary research and greater financial and professional commitment to research, and the application of different research models such as a combination of quantitative with qualitative research.

Third: Increased emphasis on preventive modes of counseling interventions

To accomplish this counselor education will need to become better informed about life span development models and develop more comprehensive life/social skills training programs. Ideally, implementation of these programs will occur initially in pre-school and early elementary school curricula with continuing

...counselor education will need to become better informed about life span development models and develop more comprehensive life/social skills training programs.

instruction throughout the first 12 years of schooling as well as in higher education and adult life.

Fourth: More involvement and impact by counselors and counselor educators on the development of better systems for schooling

To accomplish this counselor educators must take greater leadership in teacher education programs. They must become more active in pressing for changes that will make our educational system more effective for all, thereby eliminating a win-lose situation where a third of our population become education casualties. Practicing counselors in the schools must also consult with and train teachers and administrators in creating a more effective learning environment.

[Counselor educators] must become more active in pressing for changes that will make our educational system more effective for all....

Fifth: More counselor involvement in the entire health and wellness movement

Counselors need to become more knowledgeable about the relationship between physical and mental health and take the lead in instituting a holistic health model.

Sixth: Reassertion of counselor's role in career development and choice

In order to accomplish this sixth goal, counselors must become even more expert than in the past in career development theory, occupational/job changes, and vocational and aptitude assessment.

Counselors need to become more knowledgeable about the relationship between physical and mental health and take the lead in instituting a holistic health model.

Seventh: Increased scope of counselor specialties/emphases

Add to the current specialties new specialties or increased involvement in certain relatively new specialties such as counseling the aged, counseling the dying, employee assistance counseling, cross cultural

> *...involvement in certain relatively new specialties such as counseling the aged... marriage and family counseling... consulting with self-help groups ...and participation in crisis intervention [must be emphasized].*

counseling, marriage and family counseling, health counseling; consulting with self-help groups and medical teams, and participation in crisis intervention.

Eighth: Development and application of more comprehensive theoretical models

Comprehensive, eclectic models such as Developmental Counseling/Life-Skills Training that are applicable to prevention and remediation need to be implemented.

Ninth: Increased utilization of technology in counseling

Interactive video and other technology in both counselor training, small group and self-counseling/instruction, self-directed career searches, etc., hold much promise and need to be utilized much more extensively.

Chapter 3

The Evolution of Counseling

Bruce Shertzer

The task before us...the challenge...is to define the future of counseling. Gazing into the future tends to diminish troubling experiences and events of the present. When you look far into the future, persistent issues such as delivering cost effective counseling or demonstrating accountability or articulating the identity of counselors can begin to seem ephemeral. That's not because the idea of the future is threatening. Rather the idea of the future arouses a certain sense of awe, as if peering too far into it were intruding on forbidden ground. Who, in any case, can imagine the world of ten years from now? twenty? Who knows if the world will exist then? Or even counselors? "Where will we all be," Kurt Weill's plaintive song inquires, "on Coronation Day?"

Many projections about the future, regardless of whether they are based on **extrapolation, romantic thinking** or **systems thinking**, rarely seem to work out. An example of the failure of extrapolators, those who predict the future from current and past developments, lies in the 1972 Club of Rome's (Meadows, 1972) projection, based on historical trends, that the world's population would outrace its food supply. That catastrophe has not happened.

An example of the failure of predictions by romantic thinkers, those who create new life styles to change

Gazing into the future tends to diminish troubling experiences and events of the present.

Many projections about the future, regardless of whether they are based on extrapolation, romantic thinking or systems thinking, rarely seem to work out.

the system, lies in Edgar Wisenant's (1987) prediction that September 14, 1988 was the beginning of the fires, famines, plagues and sicknesses leading to the end of the world in 1995.

An example of the failure of systems thinkers, those who believe that transformations come because they are managed by humans who create the methods to move from the present into a projected future, lies in the Hunt brothers who reportedly sought to capture the silver market in 1978.

All that aside, some ideas about the next five years of counseling can be extrapolated from its past and present. The evolution of counseling during the next few years must be viewed, at least in part, as a function of a larger society going through one of the most difficult periods of its history. It is a period aptly termed by Barbara Ward (1979) as the "hinge of history," because we swing from this, the 20th century, into the beginning of the 21st century.

What are the positives in counseling at present? These, in brief form, include:

1. Twenty-eight states have enacted counselor licensure laws. That represents an adoption rate of 56 percent in ten years.

2. The national accrediting agency, the Council for Accrediting Counseling and Related Educational Programs (CACREP), has accredited 52 counselor education programs. In its seven years of operation, CACREP has approved a little more than 10 percent of the 480 institutions conducting counselor education.

3. Some 18,000 counselors are National Certified Counselors. That represents 12% of the estimated 150,000 counselors in this country.

4. The national professional association for counselors, the American Association for counseling and Development (AACD), has 55,000 members, about one-third of the counselor force in this country.

5. There has been an expansion of counselors employed in non-educational settings, such as in community agencies, hospitals, hospices, business,

industry, and governmental units. The rise in employee assistance programs has been particularly noteworthy.

6. A final positive to be noted is that the Association for Counselor Education and Supervision (ACES) has accepted a draft statement of standards for certifying clinical supervisors.

What Are the Negatives in the Current Scene?

The first negative to be noted is that Herr (1984), Aubrey (1984) and many others were quick to point out that most of the 25 or 30 national reports of the mid-1980s aimed at bringing about school reform were mostly silent about school counseling. These reports aroused public interest in education and contained many recommendations for improving the nation's schools. Most recommendations emphasized the acquisition of basic subject matter skills and knowledge for economic well being. Herr (1984) and others have rightfully asserted that these reports ignore that schools must provide humane environments, that education is more than the means to economic success and that schooling must be inclusive and fill the needs of all the children of all the people of this nation. Counselors are needed if both excellence and equity are targeted as outcomes of schools. Schools for students of all ages, from early childhood through late teen years, and all social classes, from the very poor to the very wealthy, must be more than places to develop intellectual skills and acquire information, or young people will not develop well personally.

Equity has not been a popular theme during this time of emphasis on academic excellence above all else. But it must be honored and the work of counselors represents the added ingredient to fulfill the vision of schooling in America. It is recognized that academic achievement can lead to and support a strong self concept and a fuller life. But many students cannot

...most of the 25 or 30 national reports of the mid-1980s aimed at bringing about school reform were mostly silent about school counseling.

[School reform] reports ignore that schools must provide humane environments, that education is more than the means to economic success and that schooling must be inclusive....

achieve academically without attention to and support of their personal and emotional needs. No amount of raised standards or calls for excellence without attention to these needs will make good students of these young people.

A second negative is that the Commission on Precollege Guidance and Counseling (1986) released its report that examined school counseling and concluded that counseling is a "profession in trouble." That report stated that too often counselors were assigned tasks that do not make use of their special skills, that counselor-student ratios had risen beyond a level at which counselors can perform effectively and that public support for guidance and counseling had eroded. The first two conditions have been present for many years, since the start of counseling. Some changes, at least in the area of public support, have taken place in many states during the past three years. The demand for school counselors, particularly at the elementary school level, has become greater than the supply. Money for helping "at risk" children has driven the demand and has led many school districts this year to employ people who do not have the training to function as counselors. The presumption here is that the consequences of doing that will be troubling for counselors in the years ahead.

A third negative is that little change has taken place in the persistent social problems that must be dealt with. Alcohol and drug abuse; emotional, physical and sexual abuse; broken families; sexism; racism; and poverty persist. Suicide rates for children and youth have risen. Because these problems are ever present, much counselor effort goes into crisis management and remediation and programs for prevention are short changed.

Finally to be mentioned is the uncertainty of the economy. Some economists predict that within the next two years, the U.S. will experience, at the very least, a recession and others predict even more drastic hard times. Economic hard times slow down changes

A second negative is that the Commission on Precollege Guidance and Counseling released its report that examined school counseling and concluded that counseling is a "profession in trouble."

in counseling and healthy economies enable counseling changes to be more fluid. Given these positives and negatives, what will happen in counseling during the next few years?

The search to establish an identity for counselors will go on, although it is doubtful that it will be completed in the next five years. When someone says or writes that what is needed today in counseling is to decide who counselors are and what they do, a sense of distasteful weariness overtakes me. It is as though I were starting to see a badly scratched film of a poor movie for the fourth or fifth time.

Many have suggested that the counselor's identity lies within the boundaries of personal and career development. Ivey and Goncalves (1987), for example, suggest that the identity of counselors is to be extracted from grounding in developmental theory, assessment of developmental behavior, and their application of developmental interventions. They assert that the counselor's orientation toward positive human development is the core that can be used to define counselors so that they are distinct from psychologists; yet counselors would maintain an awareness of the basic scientific approach.

Identifying how helping professionals, called counselors, differ from other helping professionals called psychologists, social workers and teachers, is crucial in establishing counselor licensure laws, obtaining financial support for counselors from legislators and other public policymakers.

The problem of counselor identity and establishing appropriate responsibilities and functions to be performed by counselors appears to be most acute in school settings. Although the American School Counselor Association in 1974 has presented role and function statements for school counselors at the elementary school (1974a), middle school (1974b) and secondary school (1974c) levels, those statements do not appear to have reached many school counselors, let alone the public at large. Some explain the gap between the ideal

When someone says or writes that what is needed today in counseling is to decide who counselors are and what they do, a sense of distasteful weariness overtakes me.

The problem of counselor identity and establishing appropriate responsibilities and functions to be performed by counselors appears to be most acute in school settings.

and reality by saying that school counselors have to make do with the world as it is, not with what they might like it to be. Perhaps in the next five years some new force, idea or experience will be uncovered and brought to bear upon who counselors are as helping professionals. In the meantime effective counseling professionals may not spend too much time searching for an identity but will simply live it.

During the next five years, some change will take place in the services counselors deliver. The direction of the change is to move from concentration upon remedial to developmental, preventive services. That shift has started and will accelerate. More counselors are spending more of their time on drug and alcohol education programs, suicide prevention programs, career development, awareness of physical and sexual abuse, death and dying, health, stress management and inoculation, and the like. Although at the present time, most counselors spend most of their time coping with crisis situations—helping people with their troubles—in the next five years more counselors will spend more time on prevention.

Changes to affirm a counselor's identity based on advancing personal and career development and changes in the shift of counseling from remedial to developmental will intensify as counselor education programs change.

And counselor education programs will change... slowly. It is believed here that the CACREP standards will specify, within the next five years, that entry-level counselor education is a two-year 60-semester hour program, with 1000 clock hours of supervised experience. Now, during the past few years, various individuals and groups have recommended that counselor education institutions must add certain courses or particular features to their programs. For example, Sampson and Loesch (1985) have recommended that CACREP standards add computer literacy; Loesch (1983) more measurement; Haring-Hildore and Vacc (1988) more emphasis upon scientific thinking and

> ...*effective counseling professionals may not spend too much time searching for an identity but will simply live it.*

> *Although at the present time, most counselors spend most of their time coping with crisis situations...in the next five years more counselors will spend more time on prevention.*

more research courses; Myers (1983) more gerontological counseling; Gladding, Burggraf, and Fenell (1987), Fenell and Hovestadt (1986) and others more marriage and family counseling; Ponterotto and Casas (1987) more treatment of multicultural issues; Ivey and Goncalves (1987) more developmental theory, assessment and intervention; Stadler and Paul (1986), more instruction on ethical and legal issues; Brown (1987) more career development; Brown, Pryzwansky, and Schulte (1987) more consultation courses; Ponterotto (1985) more psychopharmacology courses; and Gladding (1985) suggests a course on counseling history.

This listing of courses and experiences to be added could go on and on. The trouble is that when these individuals speak to their case, they are persuasive. [I'm like the girl in Oklahoma who can't say no!] And many counselor educators must be persuaded, too, for Hollis and Wantz (1986) reported that during 1984-1987, 965 courses were added and but 41 dropped. The most frequently added were marriage and family courses. Pipes, Buckhalt, and Merrill (1983) have labeled this situation the "psychology of more." The question is if you add all of these necessary courses, what can be subtracted or taken out of a counselor education program? If that question is not answerable, the only recourse is that CACREP standards specify that it takes five academic years of graduate education to prepare counselors!

The model of counselor represented in counselor education will change. The model in most entry-level programs, whether CACREP approved or not, has been that of a practitioner whose primary mode of operation was individual behavioral processes. many program descriptions suggested that individual behavioral processes were not the exclusive mode of operations because both personal and career development can be advanced (and sometimes better) through group, curricular and other psycho-educational experiences, those processes never seem to emerge very

...if you add all of these necessary [counselor education] courses, what can be subtracted or taken out of a counselor education program?

strongly once practice was started. For many years school counselors have been saying to counselor educators that the "clinical model" (their label for individual behavioral processes) was not sufficient for the responsibilities assigned to them or the goals they sought to accomplish.

During the next five years, change in the model of counselor will be to that of the practitioner-scientist. The practitioner part of that equation will continue to receive the heaviest emphasis and it will change to a practitioner of developmental, preventive and mental health emphasis. The scientist part will emerge and become stronger as programs move to 60 semester hours. The expanded time will make it possible to provide more research courses and research experiences. Vacc's and Barden's (1988) ideas that the scientist part speaks to not just research and accountability but to the application of scientific thinking appears to be charting the direction that will be taken.

The direction counselor education is moving in appears to be patterned after the model of clinical psychology and other professions: Entry into the counseling profession can come only after the award of the doctorate degree. Lanning (1988) says counselor education is in danger of becoming a clone of psychology education. Traditionally, doctorates have been earned with about 60–70 semester hours of graduate course work plus certain other experiences. Now, 60 semester hours of graduate work in counselor education earns a student a master's degree. The hope is that within the next five years this issue of semester hours, degrees, course work and counselor competencies will be clarified. Linked to this issue is the question of where and how counselor specialization is to be treated in counselor preparation programs. Some, if not most, counselor education programs have treated the employment setting—school, college, hospital, agency or industry—as denoting specialty. Now the direction of specialization appears to be changing to that of client problems or characteristics: career counselors, mental health counselors, addictions counselors, gerontological counselors, marriage and family counselors. Again, the amount of time in a two-year program to be devoted to specialization needs to be clarified. How much time, course work and other experiences are needed for preparing a generic counselor and how much to provide any semblance of specialization?

Clearly the trend is for counselor education during the next five years to incorporate marriage and family counseling as either required or optional courses, or as degree or specialty concentrations. Further, counselor education institutions probably will remain highly variable in how they respond to cross-cultural or multi-cultural issues. Some institutions will create courses, others will organize short-term workshops or other special learning experiences for the purpose of extending counselors' cultural sensitivity, knowledge or competency.

Further, as Hollis and Wantz (1986) noted in the counselor preparation directory, practicum and internship, long held as the capstones of preparation, were no longer being directly supervised by faculty. Rather, direct, day-to-day supervision is being provided by counseling professionals in agencies and other units. That trend will continue. Hollis and Wantz point out that these supervisors not only determine the major experiential components of counselor training but have a large input into who practices and how.

One other trend that will continue strongly during the next five years is the diversity that exists in counseling. Diversity, rather than uniformity, is reflected in how counseling is defined, how it is provided. Diversity is reflected among the 480 or so counselor education programs, although perhaps less so among CACREP accredited institutions. Diversity is present in the mosaic of counseling theories available to explain client behavior and interventions. The tensions and stresses associated with this diversity will continue. Therefore, it could be said that the diversity that exists represents a **splendid misery**, for out of the

Diversity, rather than uniformity, is reflected in how counseling is defined, how it is provided.

...the diversity that exists represents a splendid misery, for out of the tensions and stresses it generates may come creative, useful approaches to guide any vision of the future of counseling.

> *What is most impressive, at least to this observer, is that today's counselor educators are teaching competence more successfully....*

> *Counseling is strong and getting stronger....it should also be recognized that counselors have accomplished a great deal under what, at best, have been difficult conditions.*

tensions and stresses it generates may come creative, useful approaches to guide any vision of the future of counseling.

What is most impressive, at least to this observer, is that today's counselor educators are teaching competence more successfully—competence in responding to clients, in gathering information about the client's situation, in mastering the details of managing a client load and in producing client changes. The technical skills achieved by current counseling graduates appear to surpass their counterparts of 10 or even five years ago. Competence in technical skills leaves open the essential question of "competence to what end?" Students come to graduate education with high expectations. And yet, all too often, they become enmeshed within narrow routines and organizational grooves to which counselor preparation sometimes appears to be excessively devoted. Little time is left to ponder life's ambiguities, dilemmas, commitments.

Whenever the future of counseling is addressed, the inherent implication is that all must do better in the future than they are doing at present. Present efforts are thought of with less than complete enthusiasm. Because of this, I feel a strong need to conclude this presentation in a more optimistic fashion. This observer is neither highly disappointed nor ashamed about progress that, to date, has been made in the delivery of counseling or the preparation of counselors. Counseling is strong and getting stronger. Although recognizing the obvious fact that much more remains to be done, it should also be recognized that counselors have accomplished a great deal under what, at best, have been difficult conditions. An appreciation exists for those who have worked and continue to work to advance counseling.

Uppermost in my mind in concluding this statement about the future of counseling are lines from Shakespeare's *Henry IV* spoken by the boastful Glendower and the clear-eyed Henry Hotspur: "I can call spirits from the vasty deep," bragged Glendower.

"Why, so can I, or so can any man," replies Hotspur, "but will they come *when* you do call for them?" The transformations in counseling that we are calling for here—will *they* ever come?

Chapter 4

Forces for Change in Counseling and Counselor Education

Garry R. Walz

In our previous discussion we enumerated different approaches to futuring as well as some of the possible outcomes of futuring. Also, we sketched out a number of outcomes and effects of futuring upon those engaged in reflecting upon the future of counseling. Individually and collectively these six factors will continue to influence how counseling responds to the future—including both immediate and long-term effects. In particular we wish to make the point that whether or not counselor education or counseling programs deal directly with the issue of the future, willy nilly views and feelings about the future, and the role of counselors and counseling in that future, will have significant effects upon how counselors are trained and how they practice counseling both in the present and the foreseeable future. The new publication *Changing Contexts for Counselor Preparation* (Hackney, 1990) came out of a desire by the Association for Counselor Education and Supervision (ACES) to examine the new social and educational contexts in which counselor preparation is being offered and doing something about "charting the future" for counselor preparation.

...views and feelings about the future, and the role of counselors and counseling in that future, will have significant effects upon how counselors are trained and how they practice counseling both in the present and the foreseeable future.

Socio/professional forces are a different source of change and they are impacting upon counseling and the decisions we make or do not make regarding the preparation and practice of counselors. Each of these forces in varying degrees has the potency to affect the future of counseling. In *9 for the 90s: Counseling Trends for Tomorrow*, Benjamin and Walz (1989) focused on nine issues they believe will be central to counseling in the nineties. These nine issues include: Learning to Learn, Life Transitions; Technology; Computers and Counseling; Demographic Trends and Their Impact on Counseling; Marketing; Stress Management; Resource Resourcefulness; Change Agentry; and Personal Empowerment. Perhaps as many as a dozen forces can be identified as having particular relevance for counselor education and supervision and counseling. For purposes of this paper only five will be discussed here: (1) Counseling Research and Development; (2) Marketing; (3) Demographics—Towards 2000 A.D. and Beyond; (4) Generation and Use of New Knowledge; and (5) The Shifting Personal Development Paradigm.

Counseling Research and Development

Major improvements in counseling in our society have typically been driven by the actions of the federal government in responding to an identified national need.

Major improvements in counseling in our society have typically been driven by the actions of the federal government in responding to an identified national need. The public and private counseling and guidance institutes of the sixties were in response to *Sputnik* and the need to identify and assist gifted students as a means of meeting the challenges posed by Russian space achievements. Millions of dollars were appropriated to improve the preparation of counselors and counseling and testing programs in public schools. The impetus given to expansion and improvement of counseling and guidance led to a period of unsurpassed growth in counselor education programs and school-based guidance and counseling programs. Can we look forward to future federal transfusions of support and financial resources? Are there emerging national initiatives which bode well for counseling? Do the numerous proposals for educational reform identify counseling as a significant component of a national initiative for education? Does counseling occupy an important role in U.S. Department of Education research and development initiatives either present or proposed?

Unfortunately, the answer to all the above questions would have to be a resounding "No!" Whether one speaks of the activities of national education research centers funded by the U.S. Department of Education, regional education laboratories or basic research grants, counseling is all but ignored. Further, the proposals for educational reform make only slight reference to counseling if mention is made at all. Even in proposed federal programs for major social ills such as alcohol and drug abuse the role of counseling is peripheral; and if reference is made to counseling it is not clearly stated that the counseling be provided by certified counseling professionals. Admittedly there are many instances where resourceful counseling professionals have obtained funding for research and development programs but it would appear to be in response to their resourcefulness and savvy rather than an expression of support for counseling. Harsh as it may seem, the truth is that with a few exceptions, major sources of funding for new initiatives in counseling, particularly at the federal level, have all but dried up. Research and development as it now exists in counseling is almost exclusively a product of doctoral dissertations!

The danger in this situation is that the funding needed to promote innovative developments in the design and delivery of counseling are unavailable and counselors may increasingly rely on "old wine in old bottles" with a "new label" here and there. At a time when the need is greater than ever before, and growing exponentially, counseling is without the resources

Harsh as it may seem, the truth is that with a few exceptions, major sources of funding for new initiatives in counseling, particularly at the federal level, have all but dried up.

As a force for change the counseling research and development effort is a small light providing only the dimmest illumination for those looking for new directions and ideas.

needed to develop the knowledge and competencies commensurate with the human problems that currently exist and are only likely to worsen.

Force for Change: As a force for change the counseling research and development effort is a small light providing only the dimmest illumination for those looking for new directions and ideas. The prospects for either dramatic or gradual change is not bright. For the immediate future it appears counselors will have to find their way on their own, unaided by basic research and development support from other sources.

2. Marketing

The concept of marketing as a potent force determining how counseling develops is with rare exception ignored in counselor education and practice.

It may seem unusual, if not bizarre, to include the concept of marketing as a force for change in counseling. The usual practice is to focus on educational and social ills (e.g., drug dependency, school dropouts) and suggest that if counseling is to be a viable profession, it needs counselors who are prepared to be responsive to the broad array of social ills which afflict Americans of all ages. The concept of marketing as a potent force determining how counseling develops is with rare exception ignored in counselor education and practice (Walz, 1985). "Cars and cereals are products to market, not counseling—a professional service," is a traditional response. This line of reasoning, however, ignores the burgeoning activities of the high priests of professionalization, doctors and lawyers who aggressively market their services to the public. Their activities simply reflect the changed conditions in our society that legally allow and financially demand that professional practitioners communicate to the public and potential clients the services which they can provide which will be of help to them. In a phrase, they market their professional services: sometimes discreetly and with taste; at other times blatantly and with little regard for substance.

Basic to marketing activity is the undisputable fact that we live in a market-driven society. Market forces, the needs and desires of people for particular goods and services, play a major role in the choices available to people. Though energy conservationists and the government would like for people to drive small cars, people desire the feel of a large car and the image it projects. Manufacturers are irresistibly influenced to upsize cars after each energy crunch.

In a comparable though less recognized development, marketing forces are exerting a powerful influence on the delivery of education and the helping services. Almost without exception, recommended reforms in public education contain a provision for providing greater freedom of choice for parents and their children as to where they go to school, the course of study they pursue, and whether the school is public or private. Expanding educational options, e.g., a voucher system, is actually a means of injecting education with more competitiveness—of establishing market conditions where the deliverers of education must "woo and win" the minds and pocketbooks of parents and students. The successful schools will be those that are the most effective in attracting and keeping students in their schools, be they public or private, non-profit or for-profit.

The marketing forces operating in counseling and the human services, though less well articulated, are no less important or real. They are present in a variety of forms. First, is the choice increasingly available to schools and organizations of the type of "deliverer" they desire for responding to student and/or parental needs, e.g., at-risk students, pregnant teenagers, drug-addicted students. The lines between specialities such as social work, school psychology, and school counseling have been blurred to the extent that they compete for the same funds to offer assistance to special populations.

A second choice is the emerging "self help" approaches where individuals look for help and

Basic to marketing activity is the undisputable fact that we live in a market-driven society.

Expanding educational options, e.g., a voucher system, is actually a means of injecting education with more competitiveness....

information from peers rather than seeking the services of a professional specialist; or they may network with others with similar needs and interests. A third choice is the programmed interventions which through the use of technology, e.g., computer software, telecommunications, VCR's, and interactive computer networks, provide specialized technical assistance to persons on a wide variety of topics and needs. The point is that an increasing array of choices are available to those seeking counseling-oriented assistance. There's more than one game in town!

The most successful services will inevitably be those individuals/programs that most effectively meet the needs and interests of their clients. Traditionally, counseling has operated in a restricted choice environment—you made use of the counselor/counseling offered to you or you didn't obtain counseling. Or you may have exercised a choice regarding a counselor or a particular program but the information available to you regarding your options was limited because there was only a minimal effort to market these services. Frequently the rationale here is that good counseling provides its own marketing. Clients will know about, recognize, and respond to quality without any special marketing efforts. However true this point of view may have been at one time, it lacks credence when other attractive helping services aggressively promote their strong points. In the most basic terms, seldom can marketing turn a weak program into a winning one, but strong programs can considerably enhance their appeal to and the responsiveness of clients.

Marketing as discussed here is defined as **a conscious effort on the part of a developer to offer services/products which respond to the needs and interests of special client groups.** Marketing involves an active communication with client groups to assist them in making informed decisions that serve both the client and the offerer. Inducing a client to take actions which are not in his/her best interest offer short-term benefits for the offerer, and in the long haul are more

In the most basic terms, seldom can marketing turn a weak program into a winning one....

hurtful than helpful to everyone. Crass and unfounded emotional appeals also frequently fall on deaf ears.

If, as is being suggested, marketing can improve the match between client and services, and draw clients to a strong rather than a weak program, the question becomes, "how can we best market counseling?" Three points are worth emphasizing here. First, research has demonstrated that the two most important factors in a service's success are its qualitative superiority over competing services and its uniqueness. Attention to these two factors alone can make the difference between wide public acceptance of a high quality service or an "also ran" helping service.

A product/service life cycle is a second important factor in marketing. All products go through a life cycle similar to humans—left to normal aging a service will experience the life cyle of growth to decay characteristic of living entities (Walz, 1988). Marketing efforts need to be directed at the life stage a particular product or service is in. One of the hardest tasks is to terminate a service when it is in a declining state and rejuvenation may require valuable resources better allotted to new product development and introduction. A third factor is the potency of technology for turning around an otherwise stagnant or declining service. The introduction of computer-assisted career guidance, for example, did much to rejuvenate and bring new verve to an otherwise stable counseling specialty. Alert counselors desirous of profiting from this marketing research might well seek out all available evidence that former clients liked and benefited from their counseling, that the counseling offered special features, e.g., computer assistance not available from other sources, and was tailored to the needs/interests of different groups. It is probable that even this basic marketing effort could serve to set apart the counseling service from other services and increase its utility and attractiveness.

...the two most important factors in a [counseling] service's success are its qualitative superiority over competing services and its uniqueness.

Marketing efforts need to be directed at the life stage a particular product or service is in.

Strong [counseling] programs will get stronger through marketing whereas weak and unmarketed "strong programs" will be passed by.

...anything less than a committed marketing effort locally and nationally will spell disaster for the future growth of counseling.

Force for Change: If I were to choose one central point in this discussion of marketing it is that in a consumer era when clients have the opportunity to make choices regarding the number and type of services they utilize, **effective marketing is a must.** Strong programs will get stronger through marketing whereas weak and unmarketed "strong programs" will be passed by. Some of counseling's strongest competitors, e.g., social work, are mounting extensive marketing programs which are contributing to their successful entry into new fields and activities. Unlike many professional specialities, the public has an unusually large array of options in the counseling arena. Counseling, which traditionally has received a poor press and is regularly negatively viewed in both the public media and professional publications, is particularly disadvantaged in a free choice climate. Both local and national marketing efforts could serve the twin purposes of enhancing public judgments regarding counseling and focusing counselor attention on refining what services they are prepared to offer to whom. As we move towards a society in which options and choices more frequently characterize assistance to persons, anything less than a committed marketing effort locally and nationally will spell disaster for the future growth of counseling.

3. Demographics—Towards 2000 A.D. and Beyond

Any discussion of the impact of forces for change on counselor education and counseling must give consideration to people and the lifestyles they will lead. Population issues are important—how many people, where they will live, and the distribution by age and ethnic group, will strongly influence the type of counseling needed and how it should be offered. Preparing counselors for a world that *was,* rather than equipping them with the skills requisite for a world *to be* can result in too many counselors of the wrong persuasion at the wrong time. Properly used, however, a knowledge of demographics can assist us to utilize "lead time" to anticipate the needs and interests of population sub groups and to both prepare counselors and counseling resources so we are ready when the needs arise.

Of paramount importance are five demographics which will play a major role in shaping the characteristics of the counseling client population and, hence, the skills and the perspectives they need to bring to counseling. Knowing what it is that counselors need to be able to do in turn shapes the goals and priorities for counselor education. The five demographics and the implications of each for counseling are listed below:

Working Women

Young girls today can expect to spend the majority of their adult years working outside the home. As such, career and educational planning for girls will assume far greater importance than has occurred in the past. Of equal importance is the acquisition by young girls of the employability skills and attitudes essential to performance in the work force. A major consideration here may be girls of ethnic backgrounds where employment by women is outside the traditional cultural and family norms. In all cases, young girls need help to overcome resistance and personal hangups to developing skills and talents in non-traditional areas (e.g., math, science, business) which can hinder their entry into and progress in career tracks that lead to higher level management and administrative positions.

...career and educational planning for girls will assume far greater importance than has occurred in the past.

Aging Population

The greying and wrinkling of the American population is by now both a well established and well known demographic trend. The implications for counseling, however, have not received general recognition by counselors. Clearly, adult development must become a major component of all counselor education programs. Both the psychological and sociological characteristics of adults and their needs for counseling should be covered. Preserving the self-esteem of adults, empowering adults, wellness in later life, the needs of parents of adult children, and gerontological counseling are topics that generally receive scant attention in counselor education today, but will become major considerations in the emerging future.

> ...adult development must become a major component of all counselor education programs.

Ethnic Mix

The coloring of the American population through the high birth rates of non-whites and high immigration from both legal and non-legal non-white countries is rapidly changing the complexion of the American population. It is estimated that by the year 2000, white males will constitute only 15% of the labor force. While some of the decline in white male representation in the labor force is attributable to the increasing percentage of working females previously discussed here, the most pertinent explanation is the increasing entry into the labor force of non-whites. Two considerations seem paramount here. First, is the need to prepare the predominantly white and female counseling profession to understand the characteristics and needs of non-white students and adults, both male and female. It would seem that courses in multicultural counseling must assume a far larger priority than they do today. Second, a concerted drive by the profession to attract and prepare persons of color to become counselors at all levels and in all settings should become a priority for the counseling profession.

> ...a concerted drive by the profession to attract and prepare persons of color to become counselors at all levels and in all settings should become a priority for the counseling profession.

Decline of the Middle Class

Long the stalwart of American society, the decline in the numbers, power and influence of the middle class raises a number of interesting but difficult to answer questions. Will the demise of the middle class (a major source of support for counseling) lead to decreasing interest in and support for counseling? Will the new groups with power desire more culturally-bound, less professionally-oriented assistance for themselves? Will it be harder to attract new candidates for counseling preparation programs? No clear answers have yet emerged for these and other questions, but it is probable that the decline in the middle class poses important questions and may effect counseling considerably more than we currently understand.

Equally important to the topics we have touched upon are demographic patterns of education and housing, and the "so called" move to the sunbelt. These patterns are also likely to have important impact on preparation for the the delivery of counseling and should be considered along with the other demographic patterns.

Will the new groups with power desire more culturally-bound, less professionally-oriented assistance for themselves?

The Generation and Use of New Knowledge

As we move as a society ever more fully into the information age, the influence and impact of any organization, be it a corporate conglomerate or a profession, depends in large measure on how well it manages information. If information is power, as has been repeatedly voiced, then ready access to and effective use of information can be a major variable in the success of an organization in achieving its goals. The importance of information doesn't stop with large organizations—the capacity of an individual to acquire and integrate new information into counseling practices may well make the difference between a counselor who is providing state-of-the-art services to his/her clients and one who is relying upon archaic information and skills acquired during the initial counselor education program.

Force for Change: In viewing the role that information will play as a force for change in counselor

...the capacity of an individual to acquire and integrate new information into counseling practices may well make the difference between a counselor who is providing state-of-the-art services...and one who is relying upon archaic information and skills....

education, two factors seem paramount: (1) how quickly new knowledge is generated and, (2) how well do counselors acquire and use new knowledge.

The Generation of New Knowledge

By all accounts an extensive array of journals exist which regularly publish relevant counseling information—easily 25 or more in number. In addition, there are numerous journals that are not specific to counseling but publish information relevant for counselors. It is not the intent of the writer here to make judgments regarding the adequacy of the coverage of the topics or the quality of the articles in the journals. Suffice to say that there does seem to be a blend of research-oriented materials and articles directed toward practitioners. A substantial number of the research-oriented articles are the product of dissertation research while the practitioner-oriented articles voice the opinions and observations of the authors. Overall, an ample number of journals cover all but the most esoteric needs and interests of counselors and counselor educators.

Of particular importance for counselors is the existence of an Educational Resources Information Center (ERIC) Clearinghouse....

Of particular importance for counselors is the existence of an Educational Resources Information Center (ERIC) Clearinghouse devoted to the acquisition, processing, analysis, and dissemination of information for counselors and student services specialists—the ERIC Counseling and Personnel Services Clearinghouse (CAPS) at The University of Michigan. ERIC is now the world's largest educational database comprising nearly one million document and journal entries (Office of Educational Research and Improvement, 1990). It is also the most frequently searched database in college and university libraries. It offers an author an alternative route to journals for disseminating ideas—one that has the advantage of a quicker turnaround time between submission and printing and a more liberal policy regarding length and writing style. It would seem, thus, that the counseling profession, with a wide array of journals and an ERIC Clearinghouse devoted to its subject area, is very well covered in the area of acquiring and disseminating information relevant to counselors.

Counselor Acquisition and Use of New Knowledge

It is a truism that a gap exists in education between what is known and what is done about what is known. It is one thing for there to be extensive sources of information and effective means for its dissemination—it is quite another for the information to be acquired and **used** by counselors. Benjamin and Walz (1989) in discussing the importance of counselors becoming resource resourceful, suggest that by taking a proactive stance regarding new knowledge the time spent will be more than compensated for by increased effectiveness in their counseling. They suggest two main roles that counselors should adopt in knowledge utilization:

Self-renewal. Most counselors endeavor to keep up to date on new ideas and developments which are relevant to their work. This in itself is a challenge. Most of us have short lives and long reading lists of journals and other useful resources which go unread and unapplied. While there is no easy solution to this dilemma of responding to increasing demands for service while trying to enhance one's own knowledge and skills, it is clear that if counselors are to be viable both individually and as a professional group, they must give a real priority to self-renewal. In fact, just to maintain their competence in traditional specialties and responsibilities requires that counselors provide time for upgrading existing skills and acquiring new ones. Like personal fitness and health, counselors cannot afford **not** to devote the time necessary to enhance their psychological and professional knowledge and vitality.

...the counseling profession, with a wide array of journals and an ERIC Clearinghouse devoted to its subject area, is very well covered in the area of acquiring and disseminating information relevant to counselors.

...by taking a proactive stance regarding new knowledge the time spent will be more than compensated for by increased effectiveness in their counseling.

Counselors as knowledge brokers. People today are increasingly taking personal responsibility for their own development and wellness and relying less on others for help. Counselors are in the vanguard of those who can provide information and assistance about strategies that can be utilized or additional sources of information that are available. In this role, counselors are truly knowledge brokers, individuals who because of their own knowledge and expertise in areas related to human development can help other staff and parents design self-help programs and refer them to other sources of information which will help them to be successful in these programs. As a broker, the counselor has the opportunity to intervene in very direct and useful ways with large numbers of people, but is also able to save the time necessary for long-term counseling with individuals. Many students and adults do not need the extended time of the counselor; rather, they need help in clarifying their needs; they need to be pointed in the right direction, and to be made aware of the resources available to help them self-manage their development. More so than anyone in the educational sphere, counselors both by knowledge and disposition are ideally suited to perform this role.

Two new developments promise to be of great assistance to counselor educators and counselors in aiding them to both acquire and use new knowledge more effectively. The first, the ERIC/CAPS Counselor Education Partnership Program offers a wide variety of ERIC resources for counselor education programs, e.g., ERIC database searches, reduced cost for all ERIC/CAPS publications and workshops in return for the programs' instruction of new counselor education students in how to use ERIC, and the regular submission of materials for the ERIC database. Whether in preparing course materials, developing a proposal for research and development funds or completing the requisite search before writing a book or article,

As a broker, the counselor has the opportunity to intervene in very direct and useful ways with large numbers of people, but is also able to save the time necessary for long-term counseling with individuals.

knowledge of how to use ERIC can be an enormous benefit to counselors.

A second exciting development is the availability of ERIC on CD-ROM. The CD-ROM versions of ERIC are menu driven, making it far easier for new searchers to locate information. The cost for a search is also likely to be far less (as it is not done on-line) and faster, as a user receives immediate feedback on the outcomes of the search either on the monitor or on a printout.

A second exciting development is the availability of ERIC on CD-ROM.

The Shifting Personal Development Paradigm

Cast your eye about any bookstore and you are likely to note large sections devoted to what is variously called "Self Improvement," "Self Help," or "Personal Development." Comprised of both audiotapes and videotapes as well as highly attractive softcover books with catchy titles, these "self-help areas" in bookstores are designed to respond to the burgeoning demand for resources for a "do it yourself" population. Out of an aversion to the high price (and lack of satisfaction?) with the services of professionals, consumers are increasingly turning to resources that will help them to fix their own faucet, repair a broken relationship, or make a million. Present in all of these self-help books is the prevailing idea that the basics necessary to do almost anything can be quickly learned and that the power rests with the doer—"I'll do it my way!" In conversations with bookstore owners, the author learned that self-improvement is one of the most rapidly growing areas in bookstore sales and is apparently recession resistant—people such as early retirees, the unemployed, or anyone just desirous of getting ahead eagerly seek out each new offering.

Though not clearly recognized as such, we are experiencing a paradigm shift in how people prepare themselves for undertaking major life tasks, e.g.,

Present in all of these self-help books is the prevailing idea that the basics necessary to do almost anything can be quickly learned....

> ...*we are experiencing a paradigm shift in how people prepare themselves for undertaking major life tasks, e.g., choosing a career, locating a job, or overcoming grief or loss.*

choosing a career, locating a job, or overcoming grief or loss. Whereas at one time people sought professional assistance and with it a "prescription" for responding to a problem or need, the new pattern for many is to seek resources (both human and material) which they use to prepare themselves for responding to the challenge or need in their own way. With this personal development paradigm shift also comes an important shift in how counselors are perceived and used. The career planning and placement center provides a good illustration of how the shift is occurring. The popular book *What Color is Your Parachute* by Richard Bolles (1989) was instrumental in the change in the role and function of career planning and placement centers. This book taught the user a methodology for preparing for and undertaking a job search and diminished the role of traditional one-on-one career counseling.

Several important features can be noted in the personal development paradigm shift:

- The responsibility for and the major decisions regarding "what to do when" are made by the person undertaking the change.
- Professionals (counselors, career specialists, etc.) are perceived as sources of information and sounding boards, not as prescribers.
- External resources such as books, audiotapes, videotapes and computer software are regarded as important sources of information and assistance for acquiring "how to" skills.
- A key element is networking—connecting with persons with diverse talents and experiences who can provide emotional support as well as technical expertise to a person as they cope.

The new personal development paradigm is still in its infancy.

Force for Change: The new personal development paradigm is still in its infancy. New advances in multimedia configurations that increase the facility for the rapid transmission of data and visual images and offer the user a interactive capability with a variety of sources (counselor, computer, and databanks) are likely to speed experimentation and dissemination of this new paradigm. A shift in what the counselor needs to know and do in this counseling paradigm is obvious. It has been suggested that the counselor in the **new career center** (as contrasted with the previous Career Planning and Placement Center) will have as a primary focus the creation of networks for college sophomores and juniors involving faculty, employers, and students. The major focus will be on providing internships or field experiences which facilitate both career choices and placement based on employer and student familiarity with each other as a result of an internship (Casella, 1990).

How will this new paradigm impinge on the preparation and performance of other counselors? It is perhaps too early to say in any definitive ways. But the potential for major influence is clearly present. Certainly it will call for counselors who are skilled in understanding and using a variety of media and who are comfortable "brokering" an array of media resources through formal and informal client networks. The new counselor role will be one that demands counselors whose specialty is more that of a "personal learning specialist" than a "clinical counseling professional."

Computers and Technology

Few forces for change in counselor education have been as visible and frequently discussed as that of computers. Their omnipresent nature in society and the dramatic manner in which they are changing both the business world and our daily life naturally lead us to look for equally pervasive changes in counselor education and counseling practice. In fact, in the early 1980s it was not unusual to hear informal discussions by counselors about the "computer peril" or the anticipated takeover of counseling and the displacement of

Certainly it [the new counseling paradigm] will call for counselors who are skilled in understanding and using a variety of media and who are comfortable "brokering" an array of media resources....

...in the early 1980s it was not unusual to hear informal discussions by counselors about the "computer peril" [in counseling]....

counselors by computers. An analysis of the impact of computers upon counseling was undertaken by Walz, Bleuer, and Maze (1989) using as criteria the number of journal articles, ERIC documents and AACD program sessions related to computers in counseling. Their analysis showed a gradual buildup in interest culminating in a peak in 1985, with a substantial and continuous decline in the late 80s. Their review of the data led them to conclude that there was a considerably diminished interest in speculative articles about the use of and potential for computers in counseling. A greater interest appeared to exist for empirical research on "...the impact of computers on counseling outcomes" (p. 409). They concluded that the paramount counselor interest was not in computers per se, but in gaining information about computer software. It was as if the interest in computers as a new component in counseling had reached a plateau and there was a shift in interest to the use of specific computer software with identified counseling clients. In effect there has been a move from the theoretical, "what is the potential of computers for counseling" to the practical, "How can we make use of computers in this specific counseling area."

In assessing the potential effectiveness and use of computers in counseling, Harris-Bowlsbey (1990) concluded that the greater the cognitive emphasis of the approach, the greater the potential for effective computer intervention; and second, the greater the confinement of the presenting problem, e.g., educational or vocational choices, "the greater the potential for the computer alone or in combination with the counselor to be an effective mode of intervention." (p. 215)

There is an understandable tendency to view the computer as an awe inspiring "superpower" and to overgeneralize regarding its influence and impact. Walz (1990) has suggested that four characteristics of computers will have an important influence upon their adoption and use. First, they will generate both positive and negative outcomes—some aspects of

> ...the paramount counselor interest was not in computers per se, but in gaining information about computer software.

> ...the greater the cognitive emphasis of the approach, the greater the potential for effective computer intervention....

counseling will be performed better (handling data) while others will be performed less well (interpersonal interaction). The same technology and process brings about both the gain and the loss. Second, the use of the computer increases the visibility of conflicts between choices and values—decisions and choices are made sharper and more clearcut than they were without the computer. Third, computer usage in counseling leads to both greater depersonalization and individualization—there is an intense focus on a given individual by the computer (individualization) but the focus is by an inanimate object (depersonalization). Fourth, the social setting in which the computer is used, be it a school guidance program or adult counseling center, will strongly influence its use. "The computer as a component in a highly variable social setting is ungeneralizable because it both shapes and is shaped by the particular program in which it is used." (p. 200)

The computer clearly has the potential to significantly affect the role of the counselor and the manner in which she/he is prepared. But it is only a potential. The addition of computers to counseling and counselor education does not guarantee that the program will be either more efficient or more effective. Several considerations are paramount in redefining the counselors' role vis-à-vis the computer.

1. In light of the enormous potential of the computer, we must look to the creative redesign of counseling. There is a real danger that we will automate the status quo—settling for doing what we do with a little more pizzazz and in a labor-saving mode, but with little significant change in how we define our role or interact with clients. Physical scientists have used computer programs as a way of testing the soundness of their theories. We need to use computers to assess the soundness of our counseling strategies and to determine how we may better achieve our goals, using the computer.

2. We must define our developmental efforts as a joint enterprise. Perhaps one of the most exciting

"The computer as a component in a highly variable social setting is ungeneralizable because it both shapes and is shaped by the particular program in which it is used."

We need to use computers to assess the soundness of our counseling strategies and to determine how we may better achieve our goals, using the computer.

aspects of using the computer in counseling is the opportunity it provides for individuals to work together as a team—clients, counselors, parents, and community members—to design programs that best meet individual and joint needs. In most of the areas in which counselors work, significant others play a vital role in the movement from idea to action. *Making those significant others an integral part of the learning environment is fascinating and potentially beneficial.* Joint planning concerning the ways computers can be used to reach a variety of counseling objectives is likely to spark the interest of these various groups regarding computer use and help to ensure that objectives are met.

3. Many aspects of the use of computers in counseling create uncertainty. Is there a synergism that will encourage students to become involved in other learning experiences, computer or otherwise? Will the increased use of computers by students disturb parents? Will extensive use of computers enhance the counselor role and encourage new, higher-level personal interactions, or will counselors become mere functionaries in an automated system? What effects will computers have on the motivation of students and adults? Will they be encouraged to seek other learning experiences and more computer interaction, or will they be less inclined to seek out new learning challenges? We need to address questions such as these as we consider broad-term effects of computers on clients. Vital to the new counselor role is a willingness to observe, identify, and assess behavior associated with computers, on the part of both those who use them and those who provide them. This must become an important subject of discussion and analysis as we move toward a computer-enhanced counselor role.

4. Emerging research in cognitive science tells us that dialogue is a particularly meaningful way for students to learn, especially when it is followed by regular practice. This suggests a learning model not unlike typical counseling interactions and may mean

that subject-oriented education programs will be moving closer to the style of the counselor. This is an exciting opportunity for counselors to influence educational processes, leading toward discovery learning and individual planning and decision making. The computer may be the instrument for breaking down the massive walls of isolation erected by counselors over the years, prohibiting or limiting their interaction with other educators and the community. The computer can be the means for achieving coalescence. Counselors may be in a position to expand their influence in areas far wider than the traditional counseling realm (Walz, 1990).

Force for Change: Counseling today is still relatively untouched by technology. Although tape and video recorders and programmed instruction are a regular part of most counselor preparation programs, they are infrequently used in day-to-day counseling. The computer, however, offers a new vision for counselors—the opportunity not only to do better what they now do, but to redefine what counseling is and how it is delivered. The ultimate effectiveness of tomorrow's counselors will depend somewhat on advances in the development of hardware and relevant software, but most of all on *personware*—the attitudes and feelings of counselors about the adoption of a powerful new tool. It will require their giving up some of what they have done well in order to take on new means and goals. The most important new role for counselors in the use of computers may well be a sense of creative risk-taking that encourages, stimulates, and models for clients a change in viewpoint regarding the counseling experience and how to use it.

The computer, however, offers a new vision for counselors—the opportunity not only to do better what they now do, but to redefine what counseling is and how it is delivered.

The most important new role for counselors in the use of computers may well be a sense of creative risk-taking....

Chapter 5

Nine Trends Which Will Affect the Future of the United States

Garry R. Walz

United Way Strategic Institute

We have identified six specific forces for change in counseling. Each of these forces is seen as having direct and strong influence on the future of counseling. There are also, of course, numerous sources of influence which will work to shape and mold the future of the United States and indirectly, counseling. A particularly compelling view of the future is contained in a report titled, *What Lies Ahead: Countdown to the 21st Century* (United Way Strategic Institute, 1990). The report has been condensed and refocused here to emphasize developments especially relevant to counseling. Nine trends and accompanying significant factors related to each of the trends are presented. It is hoped that these trends will serve as a background against which the more specific counseling "snapshots" of the future can be viewed.

Following discussion of these nine trends is a presentation of 12 *Future Focused Counseling*

There are... numerous sources of influence which will work to shape and mold the future of the United States and indirectly, counseling.

The material in this chapter was adapted from an article by the United Way Strategic Institute in the July-August 1990 issue of the *The Futurist* magazine.

Generalizations. They seek to encapsulate the many ideas and images presented in this monograph into twelve succinct generalizations about counseling in the future. Their purpose is to assist counselors in internalizing and acting upon the information that has been presented. As such, the generalizations will serve to heighten our awareness of counseling futures.

1. The Maturation of America

The United States is leaving behind its obsession with youth and moving to a more realistic era....

The United States is leaving behind its obsession with youth and moving to a more realistic era which will be both a more responsible time and one more accepting of diversity.

Significant Factors

- U.S. population growth will slow but will also grow older as the median age continues to rise
- The proportion of middle-aged Americans (35-54) will increase sharply
- The proportion of Americans over 75 will increase dramatically
- The baby boomlet will slow in the mid-1990's
- College student populations will continue to age
- Colleges and universities will increasingly recruit Americans age 65 and over as students
- A better educated labor force will be necessary to increase U.S. productivity
- Businesses will increasingly offer skillful older workers flexible hours and retirement options to reverse the trend towards early retirement

2. Mosaic Society

Increased ethnic diversity, rising levels of education, a growing population of elderly individuals and more people living by themselves are illustrative of trends moving America away from a "mass society" towards a dynamic, ever-changing mosaic society.

Significant Factors

- There will continue to be greater proportional growth among minorities
- U.S. population growth will increasingly be fueled by immigration
- Alternative educational options such as year-round schools and magnet schools will be offered
- The urban minority underclass will continue to grow but their economic situation will not be improved
- The labor force will be increasingly multilingual and multicultural
- Women's representation in top positions in business, government, and education will substantially increase
- Childcare benefits and flexible hours will be more available in the workplace
- Special interest groups will grow in numbers and influence
- Technological advances will lead to greater customization of products and services to meet the special needs and interests of individuals and groups

The urban minority underclass will continue to grow but their economic situation will not be improved

3. Redefinition of Individual and Societal Roles

There will be less clearly defined borders defining the roles of the public sector versus the private sector and individual versus institutional responsibilities. The federal budget deficit will constrain both federal and state action on social problems and with reduced budgets government will increasingly turn to the private sector for assistance in responding to social issues.

The federal budget deficit will constrain both federal and state action on social problems....

Individuals are taking on a greater share of responsibility for their health and careers. People have lost confidence in the quality of the services of large institutions and will rely more on their ability to make informed decisions and to act on their own.

Significant Factors

Wellness will be an increasingly important focus in the lifestyles of Americans

- Wellness will be an increasingly important focus in the lifestyles of Americans
- The self-help movement will continue to grow
- Referenda will increasingly be held to reach decisions on a wide variety of issues
- State government influence and initiative on social issues will increase while that of the federal government will decline
- The traditional roles of government and business will be blurred as business spending and initiative increases in the social area

4. The Information-Based Economy

Major changes in the way people work, communicate, and play will be brought on by changes in information technology.

Major changes in the way people work, communicate, and play will be brought on by changes in information technology. The full blown information-based economy will take many decades to develop, but will demand that we move in new and unknown areas.

Significant Factors

- There will be increasing concern about individual privacy as electronic data banks multiply
- Electronic devices will quicken the speed of life
- Technological "haves" and "have nots" will develop in society
- A new business elite will develop—the highly educated, information and technologically sophisticated "gold collar" knowledge worker

- In some urban areas virtually every individual will be using computers at home and in the work place by the year 2000
- Information technology will become increasingly important as a teaching and learning mode
- A mobile communications environment will develop that will provide round the clock accessibility
- Information overload and a reduction in the quality of information will become increasingly important concerns

5. Globalization

The movement of information, technology, capital, and ideas around the world is increasing and leading to: (1) increased foreign ownership of U.S. firms and the presence of U.S. firms in other countries; (2) a relative decline in U.S. economic power; and (3) increased globalization of tastes and ideas in countries about the world.

Significant Factors

- U.S. prosperity will increasingly depend upon its prowess in international markets
- U.S. jobs and industries will face growing competition from nations with cheaper labor costs and increasingly skilled labor forces
- American political leadership will face the daunting task of developing a national consensus on the U.S. role in the global economy which is no longer dominated by the U.S.
- Increasing globalization will decrease the sovereign power of individual nations

U.S. jobs and industries will face growing competition from nations with cheaper labor costs and increasingly skilled labor forces

6. Personal and Environmental Health

Quality of life issues especially those dealing with the health of individuals and the condition of the environment will continue to emerge as key areas of public concern. There will also be increased attention to the link between personal behavior and disease risk. On the average, American health has been improving with the exception of the health of the poor and minorities, which will be a source of increasing concern for the future.

There will also be increased attention to the link between personal behavior and disease risk.

Significant Factors

- The practice of holistic medicine will increase
- The coverage, quality, and access to the U.S. health care system will continue to be challenged
- Issues related to medical ethics will be of increasing concern
- The AIDS epidemic will grow in severity
- Resolving the issue of how to provide long-term care will become a major concern
- Concern about the effects of technology upon workers health, e.g., computer terminals, will grow
- The NIMBY ("Not In My Back Yard") will grow as communities seek to avoid the burden of "public services" such as social-service facilities and waste disposal

The AIDS epidemic will grow in severity

7. Economic Restructuring

Many factors, such as global economic competition, deregulation, new information technologies, and diverse and changing consumer tastes are forcing an ongoing restructuring of American business.

Expressions of this restructuring are shown in the following illustrations: small firms will be created in

Many factors... are forcing an ongoing restructuring of American business.

unprecedented numbers; large corporations are cutting management layers and will become flatter, operating like networks rather than hierarchies; entire industries are being globalized and all firms are having to reassess their organizational structure and their products.

Significant Factors

- The aging population and the growth of minorities will reshape consumer markets
- The rapid pace of technological change will continue
- Small firms will continue to create a significant share of new jobs
- American corporations will continue to pare down their management layers
- U.S. population growth will continue to be concentrated in the South and the West—those regions where economic growth is strongest

American corporations will continue to pare down their management layers

8. Family and Home Redefined

Many functions that were once handled predominantly by families, e.g., meal preparation, are increasingly being offered as services by commercial concerns. At the same time, activities formerly available only outside the home, e.g., viewing movies, have been brought into the home through videos and cable. Information technologies also have made it possible for more consumer services such as banking to be managed at home and to enable more Americans to run businesses and work at home.

The family, however, is becoming a diverse institution with many single-person households, single-parent families, and two-income families. In a rapidly changing world, the family will be a source of stability, but it needs help from the outside to survive—such as child care.

In a rapidly changing world, the family will be a source of stability, but it needs help from the outside to survive....

Significant Factors

- Family households will continue to outnumber nonfamily households
- There will be a slowing in the growth of single-person households
- The divorce rate will decline
- The growth in the number of childless, married couple households will slow
- The increase in the number of male headed single-parent families will slow but will still be high
- The number of self-employed will grow
- Income inequality among families will increase with two income households gaining
- Technology at home will lead to an indeterminate work day

9. Rebirth of Social Activism

After a decade of concentration on business and economic growth, the public agenda is swinging decisively in the direction of social concerns....

After a decade of concentration on business and economic growth, the public agenda is swinging decisively in the direction of social concerns, such as pervasive homelessness, lack of affordable housing, social tension, and child poverty. There also will be less tolerance for business actions that the public perceives as harmful to society.

Significant Factors

- Family violence will remain a major problem
- Violence by young people will increase
- Home and community security will continue as a major source of concern
- Concern over substance abuse will continue
- Local issues that impact upon home and community will take precedence over national issues

- Poverty, homelessness, and poor single-parent households will increase
- Coalitions between business, government, education, and the nonprofit sector will emerge to address social problems
- Entrepreneurial activities directed at solving social problems will become more widespread

Poverty, homelessness, and poor single-parent households will increase

Chapter 6

Future Focused Generalizations on Counseling

Garry R. Walz

The nine forces which are working to reshape America will produce a different, probably a *far different* America than the country we know today. Some of the envisaged changes have a high probability of occurrence based as they are upon demographic or broad social movements. Others are highly speculative and depend upon the action or a lack of action by the public and the country's leadership.

It would seem that the best use of the reshaping forces is not as precise barometers of the future, but rather as images of the future, more or less accurate, that can be used to position counseling to have a greater impact on the future of which it will be a part. Using the nine reshaping forces and the significant factors associated with them, as well as the thoughts presented here in the papers by Gazda, Shertzer, and Walz, 12 future-focused counseling generalizations have been constructed. These generalizations are presented as stimulants to further thought and action. They are driven by needs and goals both for society and the counseling profession. Some are directed primarily towards counselor education, while others are generic to counseling. In all cases, though, they present a *preferred* future behavior, or position for

> *It would seem that the best use of the reshaping forces is not as precise barometers of the future, but rather as images of the future....*

counseling. Because they do "stake out a position" they reflect values and goals for counseling. As such, the generalizations will provoke discussion and disagreement by some. Such an outcome is passionately sought. Some of our finest moments have occurred when we openly and forthrightly explored our differences. It is when we refuse to examine past beliefs and new ideas that we make our biggest mistakes and miss our greatest opportunities. So counselors are encouraged to reflect upon and respond to the following generalizations.

Some of our finest moments have occurred when we openly and forthrightly explored our differences....

1. Counselors will need to become knowledgeable about adult development and skilled in the use of counseling (individual and group) with adults. The greying of the U.S. population with the large increase of Americans over 35 documents the need for adult counseling on a purely actuarial basis. Additionally, adults have both the means and the inclination to seek assistance when faced with important choices and/or problems. With the dramatic increase in the proportions of Americans over 75, it would behoove more people to prepare themselves as geronotological counselors. Most importantly, the failure to offer adequate adult counseling can impinge negatively on the children of disaffected adults.

2. Counseling outcomes research will be required both by those footing the bill for counselor training and counseling services ("is it worth it?") and individual clients who as discriminating consumers will be asking whether it makes a difference or not. Basic research on fundamental counseling questions is still sorely needed, but increasingly there is a pressing need for research that establishes the credibility of counseling and the desirability of schools, colleges and agencies continuing to offer it.

...there is a pressing need for research that establishes the credibility of counseling....

3. Of central importance will be the need for counselors at all levels and in all settings to expand their focus and activity beyond that of individuals to a perspective that leads them to seek to work within the family setting. It is clear that the family will become a source of stability and education for young and old. Counselors, whether they be employed in schools or adult agency settings need to be comfortable with and prepared to work with entire families. To provide for family and marriage counseling will likely require major changes in how and where counseling is offered—changes which may be all for the good for counseling.

4. **The recruitment strategy to attract new counseling trainees to counselor education programs needs a drastic new look to attract students who are: older, of color, dressed differently, speak with an accent, and of more evenly divided gender.** The typical counselor education student today is white, young, and female. While this pattern continues to produce many fine counselors, a strong need exists for counselor "matches" with older, male clients from multicultural backgrounds.

5. **Both research and client testimonials speak to the effectiveness of peer counseling and client networking. The demands for their use will increase.** Despite the clear evidence for their effectiveness, these counseling interventions are strangely slighted in the usual counselor preparation program. With increasing demand and diminishing resources, they offer a means for counselors to maintain their ability to be helpful with clients despite limited resources.

6. **Social marketing, or the strategy for changing public behavior for societal betterment, will need to be employed if counseling is to be a viable player in the contest for who wins public support.** Too few people today know about, understand, or support counseling services, primarily because too little has been done to inform them. Simplistic public relations campaigns offer little of value to counseling but a systematic social marketing campaign undertaken both nationally and locally can have an important impact upon how the public views and responds to counselors and counseling.

...a strong need exists for counselor "matches" with older, male clients from multicultural backgrounds.

a systematic social marketing campaign undertaken both nationally and locally can have an important impact upon how the public views and responds to counselors and counseling.

7. Computers and technology offer highly promising contributions to the counseling process, but greater preparation in and a willingness to undertake creative experimentation with computers and technology will be necessary for them to have a sizeable impact on counseling in the future. Two decades of work with computers in counseling has still left technology a "bit player" in the counseling drama. The real potential of technology to impact on counselors and counseling is still largely unrealized. It will take either dramatic technological breakthroughs and/or a larger commitment by counselors to use technology for there to be a large increase in the use of technology in counseling. A continued commitment to explore and experiment with technology is needed lest counseling lose the inviting progress made to date.

8. A major and persistent challenge for counselors will be their ability to establish a comprehensive and systematic plan for their professional renewal, including the updating of extant knowledge and skills as well as new knowledge and skills. It is probable that the *half life* of a counselor's professional knowledge today (the time at which half of a professional person's knowledge is no longer viable) is five years or less. Both the needs of our clients and new developments in the relevant counseling knowledge base are occurring with such rapidity that a reliance upon what was learned in the basic counselor education program (and haphazardly updated after that) will lead a counselor to be "half dead" in less than a decade. This can be a particularly unfortunate scenario if the counselor is also a counselor educator who, because of his/her knowledge obsolescence, is offering counseling students "dead" information before they even initiate their counseling careers.

The key to counselor renewal is a futuristic and planful approach to professional renewal. There presently exists a compelling array of resources appropriate for counselor renewal. Resources such as professional development institutes, counselor academys, independent study, conventions, conferences, and ERIC/CAPS workshops, if used in a planful fashion to achieve relevant personal and professional goals, could respond to the wide range of needs and interests of individual counselors.

9. **It will be essential that contemporary counselors be personally committed to helping clients gain an understanding of the strengths and benefits of living in a multicultural society.** With the rapidly changing nature of our society, including our changing cultural composition, counselors will have to be appreciative of and knowledgeable about the emerging diversity. It is of particular importance that counselors who grew up "culturally sheltered" have first-hand experiences and interactions with people from a variety of cultures. Clearly, all counselors will need to be cognizant of the importance of multiculturism and be personally and professionally committed to a continual multicultural renewal.

10. **All professions, including counseling, will be subjected to an intense scrutiny of the ethical and legal behavior of its members. The trust that people accord a profession will depend upon the outcome of public scrutiny of the members of the profession.** Recent revelations of shocking displays of the betrayal of the public trust in such previously sacrosanct professional areas as medicine, banking, accounting firms, and stock brokerage firms have put the public "on guard" as regards the self-interested behavior of many professions. The apparent "moral decay" and greed present in the dealings of highly placed officials in many spheres of American life, e.g., government, business, and education, has led to new calls for legislation and stricter external scrutiny of some professions. By all accounts, counseling has policed itself well. The future, however, will likely bring even more stringent "watchdogging" and it behooves all counselors and counselor educators to achieve a heightened awareness of the importance of ethical behavior by themselves and their colleagues.

It is of particular importance that counselors who grew up "culturally sheltered" have first-hand experiences and interactions with people from a variety of cultures.

...it behooves all counselors and counselor educators to achieve a heightened awareness of the importance of ethical behavior by themselves and their colleagues.

11. **Counselors' competence to an increasing extent will be assessed by their skill in assisting clients to access and use self-managed development approaches such as goal directed self-learning, networking, peer counseling, and mentoring.** It has been suggested that counselors often prioritize in their work what they personally do best (as counselors) rather than what clients most desire. Thus, while some school counselors may see individual counseling as their professional imperative, large numbers of students report that they want assistance in career planning; and after high school, educational employment and placement assistance. This example illustrates a natural inclination of counselors to prioritize that which predominated in their training, e.g., individual counseling practicum or didactic courses on counseling. Counseling will continue to be an important part of all that counselors do but clients who are interested in learning new self-managed development techniques that are not driven by professional counselor education should not have to learn about them on their own. By attending more to the self-help approaches for personal development, counselors will not only broaden the spectrum of help they provide clients, but will also enhance their value as knowledge brokers for clients who need information and assistance in choosing goals and resources, but who do not need extended counseling.

By attending more to the self-help approaches for personal development, counselors will not only broaden the spectrum of help they provide clients but will also enhance their value as knowledge brokers....

12. **The future will bring an increasing need for counselors to become assertive activists who use their knowledge and skills in the pursuit of important social needs.** The rising din of special interest groups clamoring for this or that program will require that all human services specialists join together in efforts to ensure that the public is aware of the potential contribution of each specialty, and that an equitable share of the resources be allocated to each. By inclination and training, counselors may be more comfortable shunning an activist role for a more passive one. However, if they are to have the impact on

the educational institutions and the communities they are associated with, they will need to speak up and act for what they believe is important on behalf of their clients.

Conclusion

In the monograph *A Futuristic Perspective for Counselors,* Walz and Benjamin (1979) conclude by saying:

> In car racing parlance, a driver is "on the bubble" when he/she has the slowest qualifying time while other drivers are still waiting their turns. If another driver posts a faster speed, then the driver on the bubble is bumped.
>
> We believe that counselors are on the bubble, that they are in the midst of intense and aggressive competition with other special services and special interest groups who are clamoring toward the inside track for money and support. The strident demands, the thrusting forward, the seeking for a way to outdo others blur the distinctions between services and results in what looks like a whirring, deafening, tightly-packed group of antagonists jockeying for position.
>
> Unless counselors can be seen as offering a distinct contribution, their bubble may well burst, and they will be bumped by more aggressive individuals who know what they are about. Counselors possess the potential to help people of all ages move into the future with assurance, to know where to go and how to get there. In the race for survival in helping services, futurism may well be the super-charging element that counselors need to move off the bubble into the pole position. (p. 28)

...counselors are on the bubble...they are in the midst of intense and aggressive competition with other special services and special interest groups who are clamoring toward the inside track for money and support.

Counselors possess the potential to help people of all ages move into the future with assurance, to know where to go and how to get there.

The counseling profession is growing in substance and stature—it need not act out of inferiority or fear.

Looking back over a decade later at what was written then, some of the same sense of urgency prevails. The stridency, however, appears diminished. Competition between the human services, e.g., counseling and social work, seems less of an issue than the need for counseling getting on with asserting its identity and transforming itself into a more proactive and impactful profession. The counseling profession is growing in substance and stature—it need not act out of inferiority or fear. What may help it most is if each counselor thoughtfully images counseling futures for him or herself. No one can give another a counseling future. But we can create our own. If all counselors are actively engaged in creating their futures, then collectively counseling will be assuring itself an important role in the future. John Schaar has probably said it well for all of us:

> *The future is not a result of choices among alternative paths offered by the present, but a place that is created—created first in mind and will, created next in activity. The future is not some place we are going to, but one we are creating. The paths to it are not found but made, and the activity of making them changes both the maker and the destination.*

References

American School Counselor Association. (1974a). The unique role of the elementary school counselor. *Elementary School Guidance and Counseling, 8,* 219–224. (Revised August, 1977).

American School Counselor Association. (1974b). The unique roles of the middle/junior high school counselor. *Elementary School Guidance and Counseling, 8,* 216–220. (Revised August, 1977).

American School Counselor Association. (1974c). The role of the secondary school counselor. *The School Counselor, 24,* 228–234.

Aubrey, R. F. (1984). Reform in schooling: Four proposals on an educational quest. *Journal of Counseling and Development, 63,* 204–213.

Benjamin, L., & Walz, G. R. (1989). *9 for the 90s: Counseling trends for tomorrow.* Ann Arbor, MI: ERIC Counseling and Personnel Services Clearinghouse, The University of Michigan.

Bolles, R. D. (1989). *What color is your parachute?* Berkeley, CA: Ten Speed Press.

Brown, D. (1987). Teaching career and lifestyle concepts: Meeting the CACREP standards. *Counselor Education and Supervision, 27,* 132–138.

Brown, D., Pryzwansky, W. B., & Schulte, A. C. (1987). *Psychological consultation.* Boston: Allyn and Bacon.

Casella, D. A. (1990). Career networking—The newest career center paradigm. *Journal of Career Planning and Employment, L*(4), 32–39.

Commission on Precollege Guidance and Counseling. (1986). *Keeping the options open—Recommendations*. New York: College Entrance Examination Board.

Daniel, R. W., & Weikel, W. J. (1983). Trends in counseling: A Delphi study. *Personnel and Guidance Journal, 61*, 327–331.

Fenell, D. L., & Hovestadt, A. J. (1986). Family therapy as a profession of professional specialty: Implications for training. *Journal of Psychotherapy and the Family, 1*, 25–40.

Gladding, S. T. (1985). History and systems of counseling: A course whose time has come. *Counselor Education and Supervision, 24*, 325–331.

Gladding, S. T., Burggraf, M., & Fenell, D. L. (1987). Marriage and family counseling in counselor education: National trends and implications. *Journal of Counseling and Development, 66*(2), 90–92.

Hackney, H. (Ed.). (1990). *Changing contexts for counselor preparation in the 1990s*. Alexandria, VA: The Association for Counselor Education and Supervision.

Haring-Hildore, M., & Vacc, N. (1988). The scientist-practitioner model in training entry-level counselors. *Journal of Counseling and Development, 66*, 286–289.

Harris-Bowlsbey, J. (1990). High touch and high technology: The marriage that must succeed. In E. R. Gerler, Jr., J. C. Ciechalski, & L. D. Parker (Eds.), *Elementary school counseling in a changing world* (pp. 207–217). Ann Arbor, MI: ERIC Counseling and Personnel Services Clearinghouse, The University of Michigan.

Hays, D. G. (1981). *Counseling and the future: Concepts, issues, and strategies*. Ann Arbor, MI: ERIC Counseling and Personnel Services Clearinghouse, The University of Michigan.

Herr, E. L. (1984). The national report on reform in schooling: Some missing ingredients. *Journal of Counseling and Development, 63*, 217–220.

Hollis, J. W., & Wantz, R. A. (1986). *Counselor preparation, 1986–1989: Programs, personnel, trends* (6th ed.). Muncie, IN: Accelerated Development, Inc.

Ivey, A. E., & Goncalves, O. F. (1987). Toward a developmental counseling curriculum. *Counselor Education and Supervision, 26*, 270–278.

Lanning, W. (1988). CACREP: An elite alternative to elitism. *Counselor Education and Supervision, 27*, 295–297.

Loesch, L. (1983). Professional preparation guidelines: An AMEG imperative. *Measurement and Evaluation in Guidance, 16*, 161–165.

Meadows, D. (1972). *The limits to growth: A report for the Club of Rome on the predicament of mankind.* New York: Universe Books, Inc.

Myers, J. E. (1983). Gerontological counseling training: The state of the art. *Personnel and Guidance Journal, 61*, 398–400.

Naisbitt, J. (1982). *Megatrends: Ten new directions transforming our lives.* New York: Warner Books.

Office of Educational Research and Improvement. (1990). *All about ERIC.* Washington, DC: U.S. Government Printing Office.

Pipes, R. B., Buckhalt, J. A., & Merrill, H. D. (1983). Counselor education and the psychology of more. *Counselor Education and Supervision, 22*, 282–286.

Ponterotto, J. G. (1985). A counselor's guide to psychopharmacology. *Journal of Counseling and Development, 64*, 109–115.

Ponterotto, J. G., & Casas, J. M. (1987). In search of multicultural competence within counselor education programs. *Journal of Counseling and Development, 65*(8), 430–434.

Sampson, J. P., & Loesch, L. C. (1985). Computer preparation standards for counselors and human development specialists. *Journal of Counseling and Development, 64*, 31–33.

Stadler, H., & Paul, R. D. (1986). Counselor educators' preparation in ethics. *Journal of Counseling and Development, 64*(5), 328–330.

Toffler, A. (1972). *Future shock.* New York: Bantam Books.

United Way Strategic Institute. (1990). Nine forces reshaping America. *The Futurist, XXIV*(4), 9–16.

Vacc, N. A., & Bardon, J. I. (1988, October). *A conception of counselor education: Nationally and at the University of North Carolina at Greensboro.* Paper presented at the Association for Counselor Education and Supervision national conference, St. Louis, Missouri.

Walz, G. R. (1985). *The marketing of counseling.* Ann Arbor, MI: ERIC Counseling and Personnel Services Clearinghouse, The University of Michigan.

Walz, G. R. (1988). The placement professional as marketeer. *Journal of Career Planning and Employment, XLIV*(1), 38–43.

Walz, G. R. (1990). Role of the counselor with computers. In. E. R. Gerler, Jr., J. C. Ciechalski, & L. D. Parker (Eds.), *Elementary school counseling in a changing world* (pp. 197–206). Ann Arbor, MI: ERIC Counseling and Personnel Services Clearinghouse, The University of Michigan.

Walz, G. R., & Benjamin, L. (1979). *A futuristic perspective for counselors.* Ann Arbor, MI: ERIC Counseling and Personnel Services Clearinghouse, The University of Michigan.

Walz, G. R., & Benjamin, L. (Eds.). (1983). *Shaping counselor education programs in the next five years: An experimental prototype for the counselor of tomorrow.* Ann Arbor, MI: ERIC Counseling and Personnel Services Clearinghouse, The University of Michigan.

Walz, G. R., Bleuer, J. C., & Maze, M. (1989). *Counseling software guide.* Alexandria, VA: The American Association for Counseling and Development.

Ward, B. (1979). *Progress for a small planet.* New York: Norton.

White, A., & Hernandez, N. R. (1988). Position turnover and volatility in counselor education over a 15-year period. *Counselor Education and Supervision, 28,* 80–88.

Wisenant, E. (1987). *88 reasons why the rapture will begin in 1988.* Nashville, TN: World Bible Society.

ERIC/CAPS

Educational Resources Information Center—ERIC

ERIC is a decentralized nationwide information system founded in 1966 and currently sponsored by the Office of Educational Research and Improvement within the U.S. Department of Education. It is the largest education related database in the world. ERIC is designed to collect educational documents and journal articles and to make them readily available through a number of products and services, e.g., the ERIC database, abstract journals, microfiche collections, online and CD-ROM computer searches, document reproductions, and information analysis publications. The ERIC audience is equally wideranging and includes teachers, counselors, administrators, supervisors, policy makers, librarians, media specialists, researchers, students, parents, and other educators and interested persons.

Counseling and Personnel Services Clearinghouse—CAPS

CAPS is one of the 16 subject-oriented clearinghouses of the ERIC system. CAPS' exceptionally broad coverage includes K–12 counseling and guidance, post-secondary and adult counseling services, and human resource development in business, industry and government. Among the topics addressed are:

- preparation, practice and supervision of counseling professionals
- development of theoretical constructs
- research on programs and practices
- interviewing and testing
- group work
- career planning and development
- employee assistance programs (EAPs)
- training and development
- marriage and family counseling
- student activities
- services to special populations (substance abusers, public offenders, students-at-risk)
- program evaluation

CAPS acquires literature in its subject area, processes the information into the ERIC database, and produces a variety of subject-specialized materials. It offers such products as monographs, special issues papers, state of the art studies, computer search analyses, bibliographies and digests. A quarterly newsletter (free upon request) features Clearinghouse activities, products, and articles on timely topics. CAPS' professional staff also offers question-answering services, computer searching of the ERIC database, on-site user services with a complete ERIC microfiche collection at the CAPS Resources Center, and national, state and local workshops on high-priority counseling and human services concerns. We welcome visitors and mail or phone inquiries.

ERIC/CAPS
2108 School of Education
The University of Michigan
Ann Arbor, MI 48109-1259
(313) 764-9492